INTO THE
VALLEY OF DEATH

INTO THE VALLEY OF DEATH

The British Cavalry Division at Balaclava
1854

John and Boris Mollo

Colour plates by

Bryan Fosten

WINDROW & GREENE

LONDON

This edition first published in Great Britain 1991
by Windrow & Greene Ltd., 19A Floral Street London WC2E 9DS
Second impression 1994

This book is typeset by
York House Typographic Ltd., Hanwell, London
and printed and bound in Hong Kong by
Bookbuilders Ltd.

Designed by Victor Shreeve

British Library Cataloguing in Publication Data
Mollo, John
  Into the valley of death: the British cavalry
  division at Balaclava, 1854.
  I. Title II. Mollo, Boris
  947.073

  ISBN 1-872004-75-X

CONTENTS

INTRODUCTION

On 10 April 1968, almost a quarter of a century ago, Tony Richardson's epic film *The Charge of the Light Brigade* had its premiére in London — an event chiefly remembered for the fact that Tony had just launched a vitriolic attack on film critics, as a class, and had banned them from viewing his latest production. Not surprisingly, its reception by those he had widely castigated in the press as 'intellectual eunuchs' was lukewarm, and the film was neither a great critical nor commercial success. It also managed to offend the cavalry regiments concerned, and military purists in general, because of Tony's insistence that all the regiments of the Light Brigade should wear cherry-coloured facings and overalls, this in spite of fierce opposition from Charles Wood, who wrote the screenplay (and who had been a regular soldier in the 17th/21st Lancers), and myself (JM) as Historical Adviser. Richardson felt that he had good visual reasons for making this decision; but, in hindsight, it undoubtedly spoiled what had been a gigantic research effort lasting no less than three years, a preparation period unthinkable in the straitened circumstances of the film industry today. Nevertheless, in spite of its defects, *The Charge of the Light Brigade* has now acquired the status of a classic, many people remembering its innumerable good points, but very few, if any, having had the chance to see it in the intervening years.

Being responsible for all the research, we had amassed so much information on every aspect of the Crimean campaign that we decided to produce a book dealing with the uniforms and equipment of the Light Brigade, under the imprint of the Historical Research Unit, the title under which we then operated; this was undertaken partly for profit, and partly to prove that we did know what we were about, and were not to blame for the dreaded cherry overalls. The result, which was published in May 1968, broke new ground in the military book field, which in those days was short on good illustrated uniform references; and in a few years it was out of print, and fast becoming a collector's piece. Subsequently, we published companion volumes on the British Artillery in the Crimea, by Robert Wilkinson-Latham, and on the British Infantry, by Michael Barthorp — both of which were well-received, but which are still available. At the same time we received many requests to tackle the subject of the Heavy Brigade, and were planning to do so until the costs of private publishing became too heavy for us to bear, and the project was left in abeyance.

We were therefore delighted when Martin Windrow suggested reprinting the Light Brigade book and extending it to cover the uniforms of the Heavy Brigade, which we have now done. In addition, following the plan of the Artillery and Infantry volumes, we have widened the scope of the book considerably by adding sections on organisation, formations and movements, and the progress of the campaign up until the Battle of Balaclava. As before, the uniform sections have been based on the 1846 *Dress Regulations* for officers, with the information for other ranks laid out in a similar manner.

Many of the people whom we thanked in the introduction to the original Light Brigade book are sadly no longer with us, or have retired, but we continue to thank Tony Richardson, in retrospect, for supporting all those years of research, even if he ignored it when he felt like it. Among others we thanked at the time were the Directors and Staff of the National Army Museum, London; the Musée de l'Armée and the Bibliothéque Nationale, Paris; the Scottish United Services Museum; and the York Castle Museum. To this list we must now add the City Museum, Sheffield, for permission to reproduce the photograph of Sergeant-Major Loy Smith's 11th Hussar jacket. The Army Museums Ogilby Trust has continued to be unfailingly helpful and hospitable during our frequent forays into their invaluable regimental files. The Queen's Royal Irish Hussars, and the 11th (Prince Albert's Own) Hussars, as they were then, allowed us to reproduce items from their respective regimental collections, and to them must now be added Major John Etherington, Regimental Secretary of the 5th Dragoon Guards. Numerous private collectors allowed us to reproduce items from their collections including the late Mrs. John Nicholas Brown, R.G. Harris Esq., the Hon. David McAlpine, the late John Nathan Esq. of the now defunct theatrical costumiers L.&H. Nathan, and Captain V.M. Wombwell. This time around Michael Barthorp has, as usual, been a fount of helpful advice and encouragement. Finally, we would like to express our admiration for Bryan Fosten's excellent colour plates, which have brought the dry text of the *Dress Regulations* spendidly to life.

J. & B.M.
1991

Organisation

The Cavalry in 1854

When, in March 1854, orders were issued for the formation of an expeditionary force to the sent 'to the East' in aid of Turkey, then being invaded by Russia, the regular British line cavalry consisted of:—

Seven Regiments of (heavy) Dragoon Guards (1st to 7th),

Three Regiments of (heavy) Dragoons (1st, 2nd, and 6th),

Four Regiments of (light) Dragoons (3rd, 4th, 13th, and 14th),

Five Regiments of Hussars (7th, 8th, 10th, 11th, and 15th), and

Four Regiments of Lancers (9th, 12th, 16th, and 17th).

From a total strength of some 22,000 in 1815, the cavalry force had, by 1854, mainly from motives of economy, been reduced to some 10,600, of which some 3,000 were serving in India.

By tradition European cavalry had been divided into three classes: Heavy, Dragoons, and Light. Heavy Cavalry, composed of large men mounted on powerful horses, were 'held in hand for decisive charges on the day of battle', and were consequently relieved of such chores as outpost duty, foraging, and reconnaissance. Dragoons were originally mounted infantry who rode to battle, but fought on foot. Gradually they became sufficiently well-mounted to charge 'with advantage', being at the same time lightly equipped so that they could serve as skirmishers, foragers, and vedettes. To the Light Cavalry were allotted what some considered the most important duties in the field — watching over the front, flanks, and rear of an army to prevent surprise; keeping the enemy away; cutting off their supplies and communications; and reconnoitring — but in addition they were frequently called upon to perform all the duties expected of the Heavy Cavalry.

By 1854 these distinctions had been largely lost in the British army, and as was usually the case, the reasons were economic. According to the *Queen's Regulations*, 1844, 'The number of Cavalry in the British Army being small in reference to the Amount of Force annually voted by Parliament, it is of the utmost importance that both the *Heavy* and *Light* cavalry should be equal to the *Charge in Line* as well as to the *Duties of Outposts*. The horses which are selected and Trained for the Cavalry should therefore be of sufficient height and strength to be capable of performing the duties of that branch of the service with the greatest efficiency.'

The American observer Capt. (afterwards Major-General) George B. McClellan had the following to say on the subject: 'It may be a question whether they have light cavalry, in the true sense of the term, except perhaps some of the regiments who have been serving in India and are mounted on Indian horses; for the men and horses of the light cavalry are scarcely to be distinguished from those of the heavy, and it may be doubted whether they would stand the severe work, exposure, and short rations which usually fall to the lot of light cavalry in campaign, as well as the less imposing and more active material of other nations.' By 1854 the distinction was little more than one of dress and accoutrements.

The Experience of the Cavalry

Ten regiments were selected to form the cavalry of the expeditionary force. Five were so-called Heavies — the 4th and 5th Dragoon Guards, and the 1st, 2nd, and 6th Dragoons — and five were Light Cavalry — the 4th and 13th Light Dragoons, the 8th and 11th Hussars, and the 17th Lancers. Only those Light Cavalry regiments which had served in India (and it was a long time since any of the regiments earmarked for the East had been there) had any experience of active service. The 4th Light Dragoons had been at home since 1842, the 13th Light Dragoons since 1840, the 11th Hussars since 1838, and the 8th Hussars and 17th Lancers since 1823.

The regiments stationed at home were dispersed in small groups all over the British Isles, and were constantly on the move from one station to another. From 1815 to 1853 there were no 'Camps of Exercise', as there had been during the Napoleonic Wars, and, except at the Curragh and to a lesser extent at Phoenix Park in Dublin, there were no opportunities for anything beyond regimental training; even that, owing to the dispersal of troops and the lack of training grounds, was a matter of very great difficulty. It is doubtful if many officers had ever seen more than a squadron on parade at any one time.

In June 1853, however, an event of considerable importance took place. On the advice of the Duke of Wellington, a camp of exercise was held on Chobham Ridges, on the Surrey heathland to the south-west of London, at which was assembled a force of some 8,000 men, formed into one cavalry and three infantry brigades, thus bringing together, for the first time for most of the participants, the various branches of the army in an approximation of active service conditions. The camp, which received widespread publicity, lasted for five weeks, and was followed by a second similar but smaller assembly in late July. Of the regiments now about to embark for the East, the 2nd and 6th Dragoons, the 4th and 13th Light Dragoons, the 8th Hussars and the 17th Lancers all took part.

In short, the cavalry force sent to the East in 1854 was a fine body of men, mostly soldiers of several years' service, well-disciplined and well-trained to the limit of barrack-yard and parade-ground, but deficient in transport and other administrative services, and in preparation and organisation for war.

Regimental Organisation

The cavalry regiment consisted of a headquarters, or staff, and six to eight Troops, formed into three or four Squadrons. Part of these were Service Troops, and the remainder Depôt Troops, the proportion varying from time to time depending on circumstances, as did the Establishment or number of men in the regiment. When a regiment was ordered abroad on service the Depôt Troops remained at home to train recruits and provide drafts for the Service Troops. The composition of the regiment was as follows:—

The Seat of War in the East 1854

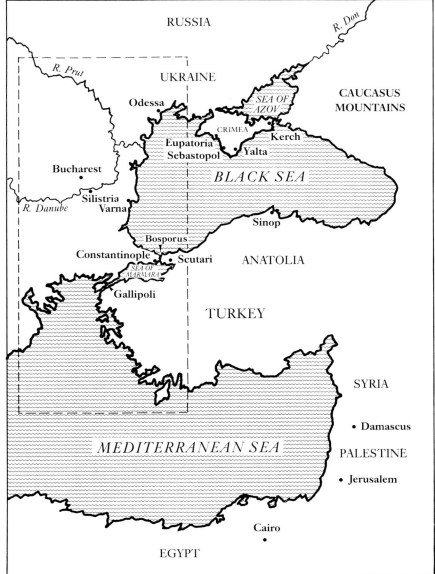

The 2nd Dragoons (Royal Scots Greys) exercising on Chobham Common, 1853. Oil painting by G.H.Laporte. (Army Museums Ogilby Trust)

Quarter Guard, 13th Light Dragoons, in marching order; Chobham camp, 1853. Watercolour by A.F.de Prades. (Anne S.K.Brown Collection)

Headquarters Staff

Field Officers—The command was vested in a Colonel, or Lieutenant-Colonel, who was assisted by two other Field Officers, usually Majors, although one might be a Lieutenant-Colonel.

Staff Officers—One Adjutant, the Commanding Officer's chief Staff officer; one Quartermaster, responsible for the supply of the regiment; one Paymaster; one Surgeon; one Assistant Surgeon; and one Veterinary Surgeon.

Non-Commissioned Officers—The senior N.C.O. was the Sergeant-Major. Next to him came the Quartermaster Sergeant, who assisted the Quartermaster, both of whom were classed as Staff Sergeants. There were a Trumpet-Major, a Farrier-Major, and six Sergeants with special duties, the Paymaster, Armourer, Saddler, Schoolmaster, and Hospital Sergeants, and the Regimental Clerk.

The Troop

This was the basic unit for administrative purposes. The tactical unit was the **Squadron**, which consisted of two Troops, identified by letters, A, B, C, D, etc.

Officers—The Troop was commanded by a Captain, with two Lieutenants, or a Lieutenant and Cornet, to assist him.

Sergeants—There were five per Troop, the senior of whom was the Troop Sergeant-Major, who in former days carried the standard. The Sergeants executed the orders of the Troop Leader, and directed the drills and duties of the men.

Rank and File—The mass of the regiment, the Corporals and Privates (or 'Dragoons' as they were sometimes termed), so-called because they paraded in the ranks, in file, while the Sergeants paraded on the flanks or in the rear. On average there were three Corporals and 65 Privates per Troop in the regiments sent to the East.

Trumpeters—One per Troop, in the charge of the Trumpet-Major, who ranked and was paid as a Sergeant. The Trumpeters were required to sound such signals as were necessary to regulate the routine and field movements of the regiment. Trumpeters from the various regiments in the brigades acted as Orderly Trumpeters to the Divisional and Brigade Commanders.

Farriers—One per Troop, under the Farrier-Major, acted as assistants to the Veterinary Officer, and were responsible for keeping the horses of the regiment properly shod.

Band—The authorised establishment was one Sergeant, as Master, and 14 Privates as Musicians, although this was sometimes exceeded at regimental expense. The Bandsmen were to be 'effective in the Service as Soldiers, to be perfectly Drilled, and liable to serve in the Ranks on any emergency'.

Departure for the East

The difficulties encountered in assembling the expeditionary force were formidable, and as a result the maximum amount of cavalry that could be put together was two brigades. Normally each would have consisted of three regiments of three squadrons each, but such was the weakness of the regiments stationed in the British Isles that each had to be made up of five regiments of two squadrons.

Each regiment received orders, on 17 March, to furnish two Service Squadrons, of about 155 men and 140 horses each, and to achieve even these small numbers various expedients had to be resorted to. The 5th Dragoon Guards had to take volunteers from the 7th Dragoon Guards; while the 4th Dragoon Guards had to take 15 horses from the King's Dragoon Guards, and five from the 3rd Dragoon Guards. The 8th Hussars had to exchange 25 young horses for a similar number from the 3rd Light Dragoons. Most regiments were forced to break up their bands and put the men into the ranks, as laid down in *Queens's Regulations*.

The final embarkation states of the various regiments, as far as has been ascertainable, were as follows:—

	Offrs	Sgts	Trmtrs	Farrs	Cpls	Ptes	Total	Horses
4DG	20	18	4	4	12	257	315	250*
5DG	19	18	4	4	12	257	314	295
1RD	19	17	6	4	12	260	318	281
6D	20	22	4		12	261	319	250*
8H	20	———		293	———		313	297
11H	20	———		295	———		315	250*
13LD	20	16	4	3	12	257	312	298
17L	20	18	5	4	13	254	314	297

* Not including officers' horses.

On 19 April *The Times* demanded to know what was being done about the cavalry: 'Are they really to go, or are they to stay? If the army is to be kept waiting for them, why are they here?' In fact, the formidable task of moving them from their scattered out-stations to their ports of embarkation was already in hand. The transports provided were small sailing ships holding, on average, 60 men and horses each, so that five or six were required to transport a regiment. The complicated business of slinging the horses aboard, and housing them below decks in temporary wooden stalls, was carried out in accordance with the instructions laid down in *Queen's Regulations*, 1844, and the *Circular Memorandum For The Cavalry* of 17 March 1854, and was achieved without too much difficulty. The 5th Dragoon Guards, 'to the wonderment of all who witnessed the proceedings', were embarked on a single vessel, the 3,438-ton steamer *Himalaya*, recently purchased from the P. and O. Line. This was the first time that a complete cavalry regiment had been carried in one ship.

The regiments sailed for the East in the following order:—

Regiment	Station	Embarked at	Sailed
17L	Brighton	Portsmouth	25 April
8H	Exeter	Plymouth	27 April
11H	Dublin	Kingstown	10 May
13LD	Brighton	Portsmouth	12 May
5DG	Cork	Queenstown	27 May
1RD	Manchester	Liverpool	30 May
6D	York	Devonport	30 May
4DG	Dundalk	Kingstown	3 June
4LD	Brighton	Plymouth	19 July

The Departure of the 4th Dragoon Guards for the Crimea, March 1854. Oil painting, artist unknown. (4th/7th Royal Dragoon Guards)

Formations and Movements

The Cavalry in 1854

The *Regulations For The Instruction, Formations, And Movements of The Cavalry* in force at the time of the Crimean War were those of 30 January 1833, revised and corrected 1 January 1844, and were only very slightly changed from those in use during the Napoleonic Wars. They covered such topics as *Military Equitation, Instructions For The Cavalry Soldier On Foot, The Instruction of The Troop And Squadron*, and *Field Movements*, and every Sergeant was enjoined to have a copy, or abstract, in his possession. Much emphasis was placed on order and regularity, and there are long and complicated sections covering the methods of forming alignments and the maintenance of correct dressing; but very little on the all-important topics of patrolling, reconnaissance, and out-post duty. The following is a précis of the Regulations, with the object of explaining the technical terms frequently encountered in accounts of the campaign, and to make it easier for the reader to visualise the various manoeuvres carried out by the cavalry in the Crimea.

The second part of the Regulations, *The Instruction of The Troop And Squadron*, starts off with a list of definitions.

Rank—Two or more soldiers placed side by side. In *Close Order*, 'the ordinary distance at which the Rear rank is formed behind the Front rank', the ranks were half a horse's length, or four feet, apart.

File—Two soldiers placed one behind the other, when formed in ranks, but abreast when marching in File. The normal interval between Files, in Line, was six inches from knee to knee; in 'Half-open' Files, 18 inches; in 'Open' Files, 36 inches, or the space left by the reining back of every alternate File.

Line—The formation in which Troops, Squadrons, or Regiments were placed alongside each other. The intervals between these various bodies were to be equal to one quarter of their respective frontages, calculated at one yard per man.

Single File—The Front rank man marching singly, followed by his Rear rank man.

Threes—Six men riding abreast, three from the Front rank and three from the Rear rank.

Section of Threes—Three men abreast, each Rear rank

three, followed by the Front rank three.

Column—The formation in which the Line was broken up into several parts, each following exactly behind the other. In *Close Column* the distance between Troops was one horse's length; between Squadrons two horse's lengths; and between Regiments four horse's lengths. In *Open Column* the distance between Squadrons, Troops, and Divisions was equal to their respective frontages, the leading body allowing a Squadron interval in addition.

Direct Echelon—The term when the Line was broken into several parts moving directly to their front or rear, in succession, thus:—

Oblique Echelon—The term when the Line was broken into several parts, by wheels from Line or Column, so as to be oblique to the former front, and parallel to each other, thus:—

Pivot—The outward man on that flank of a Squadron, or smaller body, upon which that body turns in wheeling. When in Column, 'Right in Front', the Left is the Pivot Flank; and the reverse when 'Left in Front'. The flank opposed to the Pivot Flank was termed the Reverse Flank. Behind this innocuous-sounding statement lay a tactical problem with which Captain Nolan was much concerned, which made it extremely difficult to make rapid decisions in the face of the enemy, and severely limited the speed of formation into line. In essence it meant that a column 'Right in Front' could only form line by the succeeding Troops forming up on the *left* of the leading Troop, and *vice versa*. 'Not', as Nolan commented, 'because there is any natural impediment in the way' to prevent them forming up on either flank of the leading Troop, but because if they were to do so they would then stand in line in the wrong order.

The Formation of the Squadron

When the two Troops of the Squadron were assembled on parade they formed up in two ranks. As administrative units they often varied in strength, and the two Troops had first to be equalised by moving men from the larger to the smaller. They were then 'told off' into four *Divisions*, and, if the Squadron was more than 64 Files strong, into eight *Sub-Divisions*, then into *Threes*, and finally into *Files*, starting at the centre of the Squadron, and telling off to each flank. The Officers and Non-Commissioned Officers, Trumpeters, and Farriers then took their posts as follows:—

Commanding Officer ('Squadron Leader')—One horse's length in front of the centre of the Squadron.

Two Officers ('Troop Leaders')—At the same distance in front of the centre of each Troop.

One Officer ('Squadron Serrefile')—Half a horse's length in rear of the centre of the Squadron.

Two Officers ('Troop Serrefiles')—At the same distance in rear of the centre of each Troop.

Troop Sergeant-Major, or Sergeant—Carrying the Standard in the centre of the Front rank, covered by a Corporal. When Standards were not carried, as in the Crimea, the N.C.O. on the right of the Left Troop was to be considered the centre of the Squadron.

Eight Non-Commissioned Officers—One on each flank of the four Divisions, with a Corporal, or 'Intelligent Man', as Coverer in the Rear rank.

One Non-Commissioned Officer ('Squadron Marker')—One horse's length to the right of the Squadron Serrefile.

Two Trumpeters—One in rear of the second file from each flank of the Squadron.

The supernumary Officers, Sergeants, and the Farriers, if on parade, were distributed in one line, half a horse's length from the rear rank.

Formation of the Regiment

When the Regiment was formed in Line, the Commanding Officer took post in front of the centre of the Regiment, half a horse's length in front of the line of Officers, with his Trumpeter half a horse's length behind him. The Regimental Sergeant-Major, who acted with the Adjutant as Regimental Marker, was posted in rear of the third File from the right of the left Troop of the centre Squadron. The Adjutant took post on the right flank of the Regiment.

Movement

Bodies of cavalry could move either in *Line* or *Column*. Changes of position from one distant situation to another could be made either in *Line*, by the *Direct Echelon*, by the *Oblique Echelon of Troops*, by *Squadron Columns of Threes*, or *Divisions*, or by the movements of the *Open Column*. Line was the usual formation for the *Attack*, or *Charge*, and all the different movements of the Line were 'intended to place it in the most advantageous situation' for the same.

Columns, of which there were two sorts, *Close* and *Open*, had a variety of uses. The *Close Column*, usually composed of Squadrons, was used for assembly rather than changes of position, and was useful for forming Line to the front in the quickest manner, concealing numbers from the enemy, and extending in any direction that might be required. The *Open Column* of Troops, or Divisions, was the usual formation for manoeuvring in the field, preceding many movements into Line. *Double Columns* were used when taking up Oblique positions, or when forming Supports and Reserves, when 'in Brigade'. The *Column of Threes* was useful for moving quickly to either flank, or to the rear, as the width of three men, side by side, was equal to the depth of one horse, so that a group of three men could pivot to left, right, or about on the centre men, and still occupy the same amount of ground.

The Regulations concerning a body of cavalry about to deliver an *Attack* were lengthy and complicated, but are worth noting as they are relevant to what actually happened on the field of Balaclava. Before launching their attack the force was to be divided into three parts, a *First Line*, a *Support Line*, and a *Reserve*. The First Line, roughly one third of the whole force, should be formed in Line. The Support Line, 400 yards in rear of the First Line, may also be in line, or in *Double Open Columns*. The Reserve, 400 yards from the Support Line, should be in similar columns, or in *Regimental Close Columns*.

13th Light Dragoons exercising on Chobham Common, 1853: two squadrons in direct echelon, the squadron leader in front of the centre of the squadron and the two troop leaders in front of the centre of their troops. Watercolour by A.F. de Prades. (National Army Museum)

When the line is to charge, the words of command are, 'March!', 'Trot!', 'Gallop!', 'Charge!', 'Walk!', and 'Halt!'. The line, led by the Commanding Officer at such a pace that the flanks and rear may always keep up, should move at a brisk trot until within 250 yards of the enemy, and then gallop, increasing speed until within 40 yards of the objective of the attack, when the word 'Charge!' will be given, 'and the gallop made with as much regularity as the body can bear in good order'.

If the line fails in its attack, the Officers must endeavour to prevent their men falling back on the supports. They must try to lead them round by the flanks, and rally them in the rear. 'Nothing can be more fatal than a disordered body throwing itself back upon a line advancing to its assistance'.

The *Paces* to be observed by bodies of cavalry were:—

WALK—Not to exceed four miles per hour
TROT—Not to exceed eight and a half miles per hour as the general pace for manoeuvres.
GALLOP—To be eleven miles per hour.

The rate of the *Charge* was not to exceed the 'utmost speed of the slowest horses'.

Alignment and Dressing

Movements in line were regulated by the *Squadron of Direction*, which was to be the centre Squadron, or, if the numbers were uneven, the right centre Squadron. When the line broke into Column, it was the head, or leading flank which conducted it. In either case it was the *Base Squadron, Troop* or *Division*, on which the formation was made.

Markers

The Markers employed in Regimental movements were the Adjutant, the Regimental Sergeant-Major, and one N.C.O. per Squadron ('Squadron Markers'). The Troop Leader of the Base Troop was, in all movements, placed by the Squadron Leader to mark the base of the intended line. Officers and Markers so employed were to raise the hilts of their swords to the height of the cheek, keeping the blade vertical with the edge to the front. Markers for the covering of Columns were to hold their swords vertical with the edge to the side. Markers from the remaining Squadrons were to arrive on the new position 40 yards ahead of their Squadrons, so as to be steadily aligned before they reached him.

Dressing

When taking up dressing in line the Squadron and Troop Leaders turned and faced their Squadrons, six inches away from the heads of the horses in the front

rank. On the order 'Eyes Front!' they resumed their former posts half a horse's length in front of their Squadrons.

Firing

Apart from the firing of pistols and revolvers by individual Officers, and of pistols by N.C.Os and Trumpeters (and Privates of Lancer regiments, who had no carbines), as a general rule the cavalry only used their firearms when skirmishing or when on outpost duty.

Skirmishing

The objects of skirmishing were to gain time, to watch the enemy, to keep him in check, and to prevent him approaching too close to the main body. When the call for Skirmishers was sounded, they moved out from their posts on the flanks of Squadrons, and formed a single rank, at about 20-yard intervals, covering the front of the regiment at a distance of 150-200 yards, and outflanking it by 80-100 yards.

Skirmishers were to 'level low' and were never to fire without deliberate aim. They were to keep their horses on the move 'to avoid becoming a mark to their opponents', and they were to be very exact and alert in noting and instantly obeying signals from the Subaltern in charge, or from the Commanding Officer's trumpet. In retiring they were always to avoid any appearance of haste or confusion.

Picquets

Picquets were detachments sent out from the main body to protect the front, flanks, and rear from surprise. The Officer in charge first posted a small party under an N.C.O. about 100 yards in front of the Picquet. Their task was to keep all the *Vedettes* in sight and to report their signals. The chain of Vedettes was then posted in pairs so as to cover all the possible lines of approach, each Vedette having a clear view of those on his left and right, while those on the flanks kept in touch with the Vedettes of adjoining Picquets. If the enemy was seen approaching, the Vedettes circled their horses at a walk, trot, or gallop, depending on the number of the approaching force. If this consisted of cavalry only, the two Vedettes both circled to their right; if infantry only, both circled to their left; and if both cavalry and infantry one circled to the right and the other to the left, the circling being gradually taken up by all the Vedettes in sight. The 'last signal' of firing was to be avoided, except in the case of sudden and decided attack, or in the case of persons refusing to answer them, having been challenged twice. When the Picquet was driven in, it was to retire as slowly as possible, taking every advantage of the road or ground to check the enemy's advance.

The Cavalry in Action

The Voyage out East

Most of the regiments had an uneventful, if not tedious passage to Constantinople, and from there on to Varna on the Black Sea coast of Bulgaria where the army was to assemble, while the Allies decided what to do next. The sailing transports took from three to six weeks to reach the Bosphorus, and a further two days to Varna, while the *Himalaya* completed the 3,360-mile journey in only 14 days.

The 17th Lancers arrived first, closely followed by the 8th Hussars, but as the latter were armed with carbines they were sent on ahead to Bulgaria. They were followed by the 11th Hussars and the 13th Light Dragoons, and the bulk of the heavy cavalry. Some of the earlier arrivals were disembarked at Constantinople and put up in the cavalry barracks at Kulalie on the Asiatic shore. By the beginning of August all the cavalry were assembled in Bulgaria with the exception of the Scots Greys, who arrived at Constantinople on 10 August, moved into Kulalie Barracks, and then sailed direct to the Crimea, arriving there on 24 September.

Most regiments suffered losses among the horses, the worst being those of the 6th Inniskilling Dragoons, one of whose transports, the *Europa*, carrying the headquarters of the regiment, caught fire 200 miles out from Plymouth. The Commanding Officer, Veterinary Officer, four Sergeants, 12 Privates, and 57 horses were lost; only the R.S.M. and 11 men survived. Apart from this incident, the arrangements for the horses worked well on the whole, although an immense amount of care was needed to prevent and treat the particular condition known as the 'Mad Staggers'. In rough weather the plank decking of the horse floors, laid upon a shingle base, could shift, with disastrous results; and on some vessels the partitions between the stalls were open at the bottom, so that when the ship rolled and a horse fell it could easily slide underneath into the next stall, and kick its neighbour, 'which in turn kicked and struggled until it too fell'. On other ships the water casks were stowed beneath the horse floor, so that in order to gain access to the bungs the

horses had to be taken out of their stalls, the planks lifted, and the shingle dug away. The journey took so much out of the horses that when they arrived at Varna they were particularly susceptible to sickness; thus 30 horses of the Royals had to be shot soon after their arrival.

The arrival dates of the various regiments, as far as can be ascertained, and the losses they sustained, were as follows:—

	Arrived Turkey	Departed Turkey	Arrived Varna	Horses Lost
17L Before	20 May*	2 June	4 June (*Ganges*)	26
8H	20 May*	29 May	31 May	16
11H	18 June	22 June	7 July	11
13LD	9 June*	13 June	2 July	—
5DG	9 June	12 June	12 June (*Himalaya*)	—
1RD			14 July	—
6D			11 July	57
4DG	6 July	7 July	18 July	14
4LD			4 August (*Simla*)	4
2D	10 August*			

* Stationed at Kulalie Barracks.

The 'Soreback reconnaissance', 25 June — 11 July

On 25 June Lord Raglan ordered Lord Cardigan, now at Varna, to proceed 'in person', with two squadrons of Light Cavalry, and all the Turkish cavalry under his command, 'towards Karasu, in order to ascertain the movements of the enemy'. Later that same day Lord Cardigan left with 121 men of the 8th Hussars, 75 men of the 13th Light Dragoons and a few Turkish lancers. They reached Karasu on the 29th, after a difficult march over a waterless desert, where it was discovered that the Russians had withdrawn across the Danube.

Instead of coming straight back, however, Lord Cardigan decided to return by way of Russova, Silistria, and Schumla after patrolling along the bank of the Danube. At Russova Cossacks were seen for the first time on the far bank, and at Silistria, which was reached on 3 July, forty or fifty thousand Russians could be seen camped on the other side of the river. Marching via Schumla the patrol arrived back at Devna on 11 July.

Both men and horses returned in very bad order. They had marched about 300 miles in 17 days, over very difficult country, with little rest, bivouacking in the open every night, fully dressed and ready to turn out at a moment's notice. 'They had started in robust health', wrote Private Mitchell, 'but returned mere shadows of their former selves . . . some of the horses were completely knocked, and had to be shot. Besides this, the seeds of disease were sown in many men's constitutions, and they never recovered'. On home service the average Dragoon weighed 20 stone in complete marching order. On the reconnaissance, however, in hot weather, the unfortunate horses had to carry in addition ' . . . two folded blankets, one on top of the valise, and one under the saddle, barley for three days 36 lbs, two hay nets filled with hay about twenty pounds, three pounds of biscuit, and three pounds of beef or pork; a small keg holding three pints, and extra ammunition'.

This was the first example of the grievous lack of experience of the British cavalry, for in India cavalry operated under similar conditions, without such loss of condition. Lord Cardigan's mistakes were in pushing his men too hard, and returning, unecessarily, the long way round.

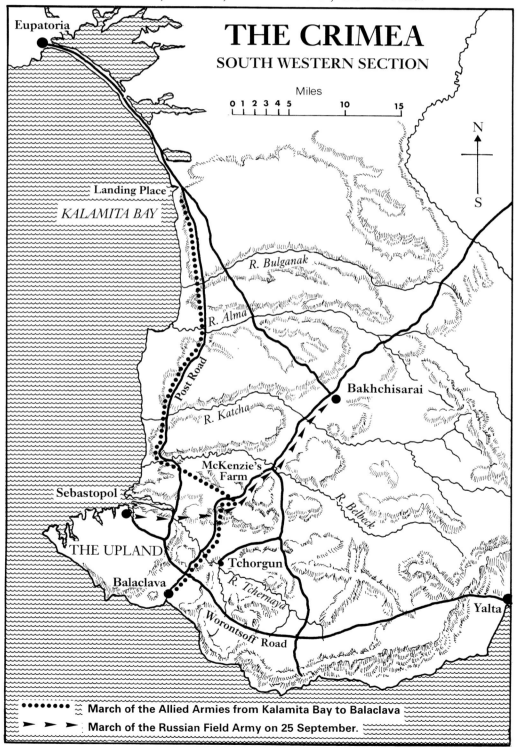

THE CRIMEA
SOUTH WESTERN SECTION

Miles

0 1 2 3 4 5   10   15

N
S

Eupatoria

Landing Place

KALAMITA BAY

R. Bulganak

R. Alma

Post Road

Bakhchisarai

R. Katcha

McKenzie's Farm

Sebastopol

R. Belbeck

THE UPLAND

Tchorgun

Balaclava

R. Tchernaya

Worontsoff Road

Yalta

• • • • • • • **March of the Allied Armies from Kalamita Bay to Balaclava**

➤ ➤ ➤ **March of the Russian Field Army on 25 September.**

16

Privates of the regiments of the Heavy Brigade: from left, 4th
Dragoon Guards, 5th Dragoon Guards, 1st Royal Dragoons,
2nd Dragoons, 6th (Inniskilling) Dragoons. Watercolour by
General Vanson. (Musée de l'Armée, Paris)

Privates of the regiments of the Light Brigade: from left, 4th
Light Dragoons, 8th Hussars, 11th Hussars, 13th Light
Dragoons, 17th Lancers, Royal Horse Artillery. Watercolour
by General Vanson. (Musée de l'Armée)

Varna and Devna, July — August

Everyone who landed at Varna was convinced that he would shortly be marching overland towards a bloody battle with the Russians near the Danube, and 'few could have pin-pointed the Crimean peninsula on a map at a moment's notice'. As the weeks passed without any sign of action morale worsened. As early as 16 June Private Davis of the 17th Lancers wrote that 'they have commenced flogging in earnest. We think nothing of seeing a man tied to the forage cart and get 50 lashes for breakfast'. Lord Lucan, in command of the cavalry, soon after his arrival held a series of 'Field-days', using commands 'so completely out of date' that none of the Officers knew what he meant. Although he was later persuaded to think again, he ordered that the 'new drill', as he called it, (actually that introduced in 1833) should be dropped in favour of that in use when he had last served with his regiment. Lord Cardigan kept the Light Brigade hard at work, exercising them daily in field movements including skirmishing drill, charging in line and by squadrons, outpost drill etc. These 'rendered the men as efficient as it was possible for them to be. But on the horses the work pressed very hardly and their condition did not improve'. The long drills in the sun, the subsequent watering parades and hot midday 'Stables' told on the men, while lack of experience in foraging and the failure to secure the plentiful grass crop told on the horses. Before long the health of the army deteriorated; diarrhoea and dysentry, caused by bad camp sanitation and the pollution of the local water supplies, eventually gave place to cholera, brought to Bulgaria on the French ships from Marseilles.

The retreat of the Russians from the Danube after their failure to take Silistria, and their defeat at Giurgevo in July, had achieved the object of the war — the withdrawal of the Russians from Turkish territory — without the intervention of the Allies. Nevertheless the respective governments decided to divert the expeditionary force to the Crimea, with the intention of taking Sebastopol, Russia's great naval base in the Black Sea.

The Landing in the Crimea, 14 and 15 September

At the end of August orders were issued to prepare for the embarkation, and on 7 September the British flotilla left Varna to meet up with the French and Turkish contingents which were already at sea. The Order of Battle of the British cavalry, first mentioned in General Orders on 2 May, was as follows:—

Major-General The Earl of Lucan commanding the Cavalry Division. He wears a general officer's frock coat and booted overalls. Among his decorations he wears the Russian Order of St Anne awarded for his service with the Russian Army in the Russo-Turkish war of 1828-29. Mezzotint after Sir Francis Grant. (National Army Museum)

Cavalry Division
Major-General The Earl of Lucan

1st Brigade of Cavalry—*Brigadier-General the Earl of Cardigan, 11th Hussars*
4th Light Dragoons
8th Hussars
11th Hussars
13th Light Dragoons
17th Lancers

2nd Brigade of Cavalry—*Brigadier-General The Honble J.Y. Scarlett, 5th D.Gds.*
4th Dragoon Guards
5th Dragoon Guards
1st Royal Dragoons
2nd Royal North British Dragoons
6th Inniskilling Dragoons

It was the decision to invade the Crimea which had prompted the sending out of two additional regiments, the 4th Light Dragoons and the Scots Greys, the second of which was still at Kulalie Barracks at Constantinople. On 24 August the artillery was distributed among the various Divisions, I Troop, Royal Horse Artillery (Captain G.A. Maude) being assigned to the Cavalry Division.

There were not enough transports, and the troops were terribly crowded for the seven-day voyage. Tents, baggage, animals, and stores of every sort, including the ambulances and the regimental medicine chests, had to be left behind. The four regiments of heavy cavalry were also left behind. Cholera continued unabated among the crowded shipping, and many men were buried at sea. By the time they landed in the Crimea the 8th Hussars had lost 95 men from sickness and death in three and a half months.

The place chosen by Lord Raglan for the landing was a strip of open beach 20 miles south of Eupatoria and 30 miles north of Sebastopol. The procedure for the disembarkation, which began on 14 September, was based on the last recorded precedent, that of General Abercromby's landing at Aboukir in 1801; but thanks to the efforts of the Royal Navy, and the absence of Russian opposition, it was carried out with minimal casualties. Most of the cavalry landed on the following day, slinging their horses into long flat-bottomed boats, and then, as the boats could not get right inshore, pushing them overboard some distance out and making them swim ashore. The men landed with a full amount of ammunition, water, and three days' cooked provisions; nevertheless the condition of the army was, thanks to the weather and the total lack of good staff work, 'pitiable in the extreme . . . Destitution and disorder reigned in the British Camp so far as any arrangements were concerned

that were not directly military'.

On the morning of the 18th the army was ready to start on the march to Sebastopol, but first a Troop of the 11th Hussars was sent forward on a reconnaissance. On coming across several troops of Cossacks similarly engaged it was forced to withdraw. However, the Hussars, 'thanks to the liberality of Lord Cardigan, and not to the "regulation price" of British cavalry horses, were admirably mounted, and they literally played with the Cossacks, as the latter, on their rough-looking, but sturdy and agile little horses, attempted pursuit'.

The Bulganak Affair, 19 September

The whole army now advanced, covered by the 11th Hussars in extended skirmishing order; and on the afternoon of 19 September reached the River Bulganak, a small stream, with a bridge and post house where it was crossed by the main road to Sebastopol. The country was bare and treeless, and on the far side of the river the ground rose in a series of undulations on which could be seen bodies of Cossacks. Lord Cardigan was ordered forward to reconnoitre with the 11th and 13th, who trotted on for two miles or so in 'Column of Troops' until they came in sight of the Russian skirmishers, throwing off their hay-nets to free themselves for fighting. Half of the left Troop of the 11th and half of the right Troop of the 13th were now sent out as skirmishers, and the first shots of the campaign were exchanged. There is some argument as to how effective this exchange of fire was, one account claiming that the Russians lost 25 men and 35 horses. According to Sergeant-Major Smith of the 11th, his regiment 'principally inflicted this loss, for being so well-mounted, they rode in very small detachments near to the Cossacks and fired, retiring with impunity'.

While this was going on, some 6,000 Russian infantry could be seen moving up the reverse of the second rise, out of sight of Lord Cardigan, who had now been joined by Lord Lucan, and Lord Raglan sent General Airey to order the cavalry to retire. After some discussion he persuaded the two Lords to comply, and the bugles sounded 'Retire by Alternate Squadrons'. The 13th sounded 'Rally to the Left', and the Adjutant gave the order 'Threes right, leading Threes right wheel', leading the skirmishers back to their regiment. The two regiments then retired at the Walk, each pair of squadrons retiring about 100 yards, fronting, and halting, while the other pair passed through them. The Russians now also retired, uncovering some horse artillery which opened fire, causing the first four British casualties of the campaign. The 11th now inclined to their left, and the 13th to their right, thus clearing the front of 'I' Troop R.H.A. which opened fire, whereupon all the Russians retreated. According to Private Gregory of the 13th, his regiment lost four men and five horses wounded in this affair; he was lucky to survive himself, as his sword was bent double in his hand by a Russian ball.

McKenzie's Farm, 25 September

The Battle of the Alma took place on the following day, but apart from an attempt to pursue the retreating enemy at the end of the day, which was called off by Lord Raglan, much to their disgust, the light cavalry took no part in the action. On the 24th the Scots Greys arrived from Constantinople and disembarked at the Katcha River at the rear of the army. Being the freshest troops available they were rapidly passed up to the front, so that they were present at the next 'affair'.

Lord Raglan, having 'been obliged in deference to the French' to abandon his plan of attacking Sebastopol from the north, decided to move the army around the fortress, inland, from north to south. On 25 September the so-called 'Flank March' commenced, the first part of the route laying through oak coppice and thick undergrowth which was difficult for the artillery, in particular, to negotiate.

Lord Lucan, with the cavalry and 'C' and 'I' Troops, R.H.A., was ordered to push ahead as far as McKenzie's Farm, the former home of the Scottish engineer who had built the dockyard at Sebastopol in the 18th century, which was half way to Balaclava, the ultimate destination of the army. So inefficient were the outposts on both sides that Lucan took a wrong turning, and the first to arrive at the farm were Lord Raglan and his escort troop of the 8th Hussars, just as the rearguard of the Russian army, also executing a flank march across the British front, was passing. The British Commander-in-Chief was in great danger of being captured, while the Russians, equally surprised and believing they were being attacked in force, hurried on their way. Raglan was saved by the arrival of 'I' Troop, who opened fire on the fast-disappearing enemy, by his 8th Hussar escort, and by the newly-arrived Scots Greys, who, dismounting two men out of each 'Three', skirmished through the woods, capturing some waggons and a few prisoners.

Meanwhile, Lucan and the rest of the cavalry were blundering about on the wrong road and, in strict adherence with the regulations, were marching on one road, strung out in an advance guard formation, thus leaving all the other roads and the whole country around the line of march unwatched and unexplored. Much later in the day when the 4th Light Dragoons, acting as rearguard to the army, were sent forward to blow up some abandoned Russian ammunition waggons, they discovered some 10,000 Russians encamped in a valley about three miles away. So defective was the outpost service that two large armies, complete with baggage, managed to cross each other's path, actually coming into contact at one point, without discovering each other's designs, and without the cavalry coming together. The whole episode demonstrated the inexperience of the cavalry officers on both sides in a most important part of their duty.

The Cavalry Division at Balaclava, 25 September—25 October

Some of the transports that had carried the army to the Crimea returned to Varna, and between the 22nd and 27th embarked the four remaining regiments of heavy cavalry. No sooner were they at sea, however, than a violent storm blew up and the flotilla was scattered in all directions, part of it reassembling off Sebastopol on 30 September, and disembarking its men and horses at Balaclava by 4 October. The 4th and 5th Dragoon Guards, on the steamers *Simla* and *Jason*, got off relatively lightly, the former losing only 15 horses. The Royals fared the worst of all, one of their transports having to run before the storm back to the Bosphorus, where the surviving 11 out of 110 horses were landed. The men were transferred to a steamer and arrived at Balaclava on 4 October. One of the Inniskillings' two transports, the *Warcloud*, having thrown 75 horses overboard, returned to Varna, eventually arriving at Balaclava with only six horses on board. In all, the disastrous 40-hour journey cost the Heavy Brigade some 226 troop horses and chargers. The Inniskillings could mount only 130 men, and the Royals needed 75 horses from the Light Brigade to enable them to mount their second squadron.

The allied armies were now encamped on a large plateau, facing north, and preparing for the first bombardment of Sebastopol. Some four miles to the rear lay the small town and harbour of Balaclava, through which all the British supplies had to pass. From the head of the harbour, stretching away to the north-east towards the Tchernaya River, was a grassy undulating plain, five miles by two; and somewhere beyond the river, on the open flank of the British, lay the Russian field army last seen escaping from Sebastopol. The plain itself lay half a mile north of Balaclava, and was divided longitudinally by a ridge of low hillocks extending west for nearly three miles from the village of Kamara. Along this ridge, known as the Causeway Heights, ran the 'Worontsoff Road' for some two miles, when it turned north-west and, cutting the angle of the northern plain, climbed up to the plateau. In front of Kamara, and joined to it by a narrow neck, stood a knoll some 500 feet high called Canrobert's Hill. On this knoll and along the Causeway Heights were distributed several battalions of Turks, who at once commenced constructing six 'redoubts', the first four of which were armed with British 12-pounder iron guns manned by Turkish gunners, each with an N.C.O. from the Royal Artillery.

*Major-General The Earl of Cardigan commanding the
Light Cavalry Brigade. He is depicted leading the charge in
the uniform of his former regiment, the 11th Hussars.
Stipple engraving after A.F.de Prades. (National Army
Museum)*

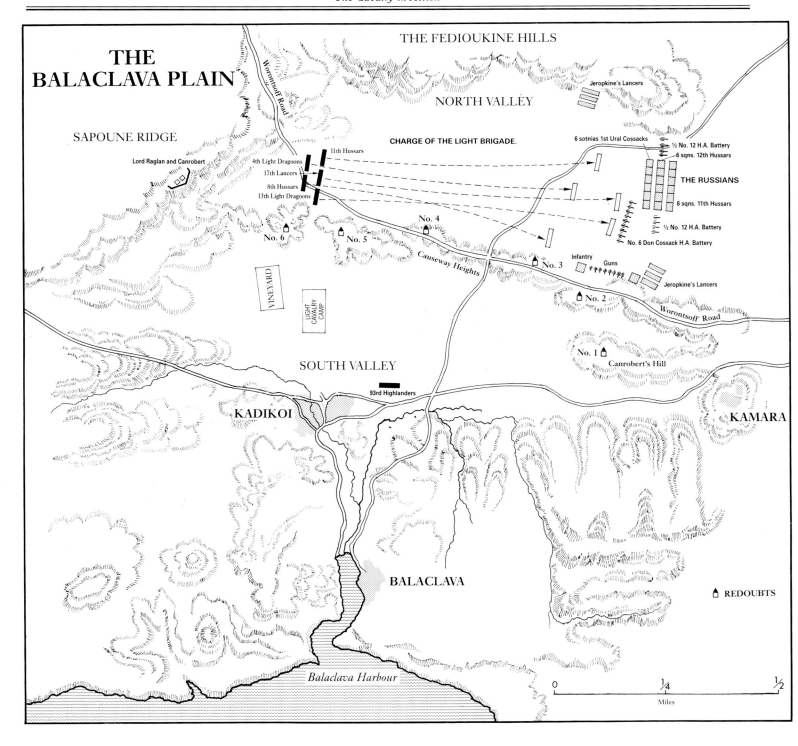

THE
BALACLAVA PLAIN

Once the Cavalry had settled in the south plain, or valley, near the village of Kadikoi, the heavy cavalry took its share of outpost and picquet duty, their main task being to protect the rear of the army while it worked day and night on preparations for the siege. This meant patrolling north-eastwards towards the Tchernaya, keeping a look-out for any relieving force. As early as 5 October they began to encounter enemy patrols, but the Russians tended to keep away, except when, as on 7 October, Cornet Fisher-Rowe of the 4th Dragoon Guards with a party of ten men was surprised by a large body of Russian lancers, and was 'obliged to retire'. The horses, without water for 24 hours, were very weak, and could hardly canter. Three men were cut off and 'speared in the most merciless manner', one being killed and the other two taken prisoner. The rest of the party managed to hold off the lancers until the rest of the cavalry arrived. On another occasion a Sergeant of the 13th Light Dragoons was cut off on the wrong side of the Tchernaya and taken prisoner.

The cavalry were soon moved forward from their first camp, and by 15 October were concentrated south of

No.6 Redoubt, the Light Brigade to the east, and the Heavy Brigade to the south of a large vineyard. The work was 'sharp', the whole Division, including the Artillery, getting on parade every morning from one hour before sunrise to one hour after. The constant calls to 'Turn out immediately' and 'Boots and Saddles' meant that the whole camp had to be packed up each time, the men often returning to find no food available. At night the weather was getting very cold, which was hard on the mounted vedettes.

Strong patrols, typically consisting of an Officer, Sergeant, and 15 men, were sent out daily towards the Tchernaya, and through the defile leading to the valley of the Baidar, with orders to watch the movements of the enemy, and to bring into camp all transport, cattle, and supplies that might be met with in the neighbouring villages. Each day the picquets placed vedettes on the crest of the Causeway Heights, facing east, about a mile apart, extending to the right as far as the village of Kamara, with a dismounted man between each vedette and the main picquet to pass on any signals. At night the vedettes were withdrawn into the plain behind the Turkish redoubts, where it was easier to see anyone approaching, silhouetted against the skyline.

As early as 13 October the Russian General Liprandi had started to concentrate his troops near the village of Tchorgoun, a mile or so beyond the Tchernaya, and by 23 October, when the whole Cavalry Division was turned out yet again, his force had reached a total of 17 battalions of infantry, 16 squadrons of cavalry, 10 *sotnias* of Cossacks (roughly the equivalent of 10 squadrons), and 52 guns. They appeared to the British front during the afternoon, and manoeuvred about for some time, but retired when fired upon by the guns in the Turkish redoubts and by the Horse Artillery. It was yet another false alarm.

Balaclava, 25 October: the opening moves

The Cavalry Division was standing to as usual when, shortly before dawn, the Russians began an assault on the eastern end of the line of redoubts. Lord Lucan immediately assembled the cavalry and 'I' Troop, R.H.A., at the end of the South Valley below the redoubts, to provide moral, and if necessary material support to the Turks, 'I' Troop moving up the the crest of the heights and opening fire on the advancing enemy. The Russians, however, soon carried Redoubt No.1 (Canrobert's Hill) at the point of the bayonet, killing some 170 Turks, whereupon the occupants of the others took to their heels and came streaming back towards Balaclava, some of them forming up on either side of the 93rd Highlanders, who occupied a knoll covering the approach to the harbour. An urgent request for help was now sent to

the nearest infantry Division, and the cavalry, who were now too exposed and suffering casualties from the Russian artillery, were withdrawn to the western end of the valley, retiring slowly in echelon of columns. They halted for a short while near Kadikoi, where 'I' Troop took the opportunity to replenish its ammunition, and afterwards moved up towards the Causeway Heights, taking ground to their left. The Light Brigade ended up immediately under the western end of the ridge, and the Heavy Brigade on the southern slopes where it was in a good position to threaten the flank of any Russian advance towards Balaclava. The enemy, meanwhile, occupied Redoubts 1-4, and finding the guns spiked by the British N.C.O.s, called up more of their artillery.

There followed a lull of about an hour; and then General Liprandi pushed forward his cavalry, consisting of the 11th and 12th Hussars and several *sotnias* of Cossacks accompanied by horse artillery, down the North Valley. Almost immediately four Squadrons of the Russian 11th Hussars wheeled to their left and crossed the Causeway Heights towards Balaclava, but were seen off by two smart vollies from the 93rd — an action later celebrated as the 'Thin Red Streak'.

The Charge of the Heavy Brigade

Lord Raglan, from his vantage point on the edge of the 'Upland' overlooking the western end of the plain, now ordered Lord Lucan to detach eight Squadrons of heavy dragoons towards Balaclava 'to support the Turks, who are wavering'. Accordingly — just as, unbeknown to him, some 1,700 Russian cavalry were moving down the North Valley — Scarlett started the Heavy Brigade in the opposite direction, back towards Kadikoi, in two parallel columns. The left column, that nearest the Causeway Heights, was in Open Column of Troops, the second Squadron of the Inniskillings leading, followed by the Scots Greys. The right column, marching in Threes, consisted of the first Squadron of the Inniskillings, followed at some distance by the 5th Dragoon Guards. Further behind, and to the right, were the two Squadrons of the 4th Dragoon Guards, while the two Squadrons of the Royals were left behind on the original position.

The Cavalry Division had omitted to post any scouts on the Causeway Heights, nor did the eight Squadrons now marching southwards have any flankers pushing along the heights, so it was a complete surprise to them when they suddenly saw the Russians appearing over the crest of the Heights between Redoubts 3 and 4. Perhaps the Russians were just as surprised, for they halted about 400 yards down the slope and threw out a screen of Cossacks to either flank, at the same time opening fire with their horse artillery. The Russian formation was roughly square, on

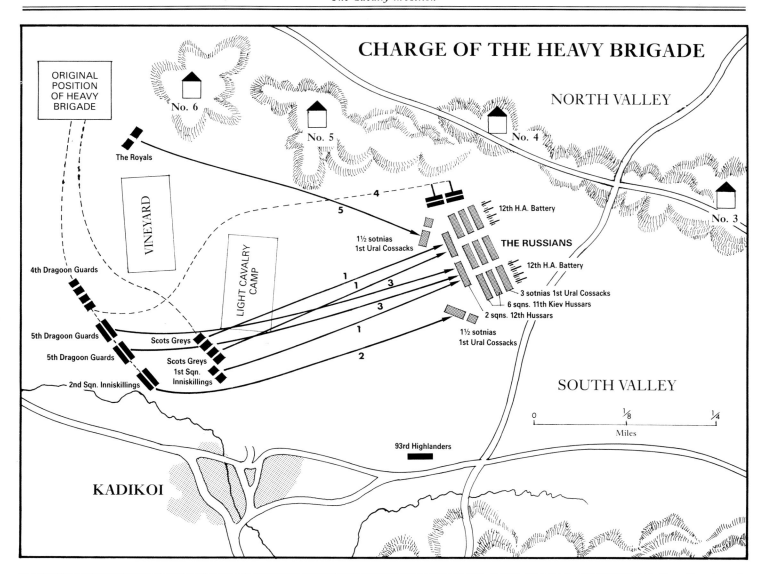

CHARGE OF THE HEAVY BRIGADE

ORIGINAL POSITION OF HEAVY BRIGADE

NORTH VALLEY

No. 6

No. 5

No. 4

No. 3

The Royals

12th H.A. Battery

VINEYARD

4

5

1½ sotnias 1st Ural Cossacks

THE RUSSIANS

12th H.A. Battery

LIGHT CAVALRY CAMP

4th Dragoon Guards

1

1   3

3 sotnias 1st Ural Cossacks

6 sqns. 11th Kiev Hussars

5th Dragoon Guards

Scots Greys

3

2 sqns. 12th Hussars

5th Dragoon Guards

Scots Greys
1st Sqn.
Inniskillings

1

1½ sotnias
1st Ural Cossacks

2

2nd Sqn. Inniskillings

SOUTH VALLEY

0   ⅛   ¼
Miles

93rd Highlanders

KADIKOI

Brigadier-General The Hon. James Yorke Scarlett commanding the Heavy Cavalry Brigade. He stands in front of his brigade wearing an unorthodox dragoon helmet and general officer's frock coat. Oil painting by Sir Francis Grant. (5th Royal Inniskilling Dragoon Guards)

Inniskilling Dragoons. 25th Octr 1854 (Balaclava); coloured lithograph after A.F.de Prades. (National Army Museum)

a three-squadron frontage, with the Hussars in the front and the Cossacks in the rear and on the flanks.

As they emerged from behind the same vineyard around which the remains of the cavalry camps were still standing, Scarlett turned to the leading Inniskilling Squadron and asked 'Are you right in front?', a question necessitated by the so-called 'Pivot Problem'. On being answered in the affirmative Scarlett gave the order 'Left Wheel into Line!'; but finding that the 5th Dragoon Guards were not clear of the vineyard, he ordered the line to take ground to its right, after which he wheeled into line again, and turning to his Trumpeter ordered him to sound the 'Charge!'. Before they moved, however, to the apparent amazement of the Russians and the fury of Lord Lucan, the commanding officers insisted on dressing their Regiments, the officers calmly turning their backs to the enemy and facing their Troops, as laid down in the regulations.

As the first line moved off the Scots Greys, on the left, got entangled in the remains of the Light Brigade camp, and the Inniskillings were forced to slow down to keep in line with them; so that when they reached the Russians, Scarlett and his staff were some yards in advance of the main body, which, riding knee to knee, outnumbered and outflanked by Cossacks, flung itself into the grey-coated mass. As the lines met the seemingly impregnable Russian front shifted uneasily as each man sidestepped to avoid the thundering mass coming straight at them; but once the momentum of the charge had been stopped it became a hand-to-hand affair, with the British hacking away without much apparent effect at the heavy great-coats and stout shakos of their opponents.

Just as it seemed that the first line would be swallowed up, the first Squadron of the Inniskillings, on the right of the second line, hit the Cossacks on the Russian left, who had come so far round in their encircling movement that they now presented their backs to the second line. The Inniskillings charged with such force that they crumpled the Cossacks up, and tore through them into the mêlée. A few seconds later the 5th Dragoon Guards, who had also been held up in the Light Brigade camp, hit the Russian front and joined in the fray.

It was now the turn of the 4th Dragoon Guards who, advancing rapidly in Open Column of Troops, swung round the bottom of the vineyard, and trotted up between it and the Light Brigade camp until they reached the right flank of the Russian mass, when they wheeled into line and charged in. The Greys, meanwhile, had succeeded in forcing their way through the Russians and, turning about, were cutting their way back to the centre again when the Royals, having left their reserve position, and without waiting to form line properly, hurled themselves against the right front corner of the Russians, which was

about to encircle the 5th Dragoon Guards. Suddenly the Russians, under attack from three sides, shifted and gave way slightly. Slight as it was, this movement was enough; and the whole mass broke and fled back over the Heights, and down the North Valley to their starting point. Although some way off, they passed across the front of the Light Brigade, who were impatient to pursue them, but were restrained by Lord Cardigan, who claimed that he was under orders not to move from his position.

The casualties in this admirably conducted operation were not heavy. The total losses of the Heavy Brigade for the whole day, which included those lost during the Russian attack on the redoubts earlier in the day, and when supporting the Light Brigade later on, were one officer and nine men killed, and 11 officers and 87 men wounded. The Russians probably lost 40 or 50 men killed, 'besides wounded', in an action that had lasted little more than ten minutes. The Russian cavalry remained shaken and unable to stand up to British cavalry during the remainder of the battle.

The Charge of the Light Brigade

It was now about 9.30 a.m. The Russians consolidated their positions around Redoubts 1-3, while their cavalry halted and reformed behind the protection of a battery of Don Cossack Horse Artillery. An hour later the British 1st and 4th Divisions started to arrive from the Upland, and began pushing forward towards the Russian positions. Ordered by Lord Raglan to 'advance and take any opportunity to recover the heights', Lord Lucan assumed that he was to support an infantry attack and contented himself with moving the Light Brigade up the North Valley as far as No.4 Redoubt, the Heavy Brigade following in their right rear. This was still the position just before midday when Lord Raglan, from his elevated position, could see Russian artillery teams moving forward, and jumped to the conclusion that they were about to make off with the British guns abandoned in the redoubts. He therefore ordered his Quartermaster-General Airey to send the following order to Lord Lucan:— 'Lord Raglan wishes the Cavalry to advance rapidly to the front, follow the enemy and try to prevent the enemy carrying away the guns. Troop Horse Artillery may accompany. French cavalry is on your left. Immediate.'

On his receiving this order from the hands of Captain Nolan, the only guns that Lucan could see were those attached to the Russian cavalry, now at the far end of the North Valley. His request for clarification drew from Nolan the impatient outburst, 'There, my Lord, are your guns; there are the enemy!', accompanied by a sweep of the arm which took in the greater part of the Russian position. Lucan passed the order to Lord Cardigan, who, accepting it with a philosophical, 'Well, here goes the last of the Brudenells', took his place at the head of the Light Brigade. This was formed up in three lines, as laid down in the regulations, the *First Line* consisting of the 13th Light Dragoons on the right and the 17th Lancers on the left. The 11th Hussars, who had originally been on the left of the first line, were pulled back to form the *Support Line*, because the valley was felt to be too narrow, and consequently overlapped the 17th Lancers slightly. The *Reserve* was formed by the 8th Hussars (less one Troop which was doing duty as Lord Raglan's escort) on the right, with the 4th Light Dragoons on their left. As the Brigade broke from a walk into a trot, Nolan, who was riding with the 17th Lancers, the right hand Squadron of which was acting as the *Squadron of Direction*, spurred his horse forward, apparently realising too late that Lord Cardigan, instead of veering to his right and attacking the redoubts, was heading straight down the valley into certain death. As he tried to attract his attention he was hit by one of the first Russian rounds and, falling to the ground, was ridden over by the rest of the Brigade.

The first line, fired at from all sides, reached the Russian guns at the end of the North Valley, and began disposing of the artillerymen. The support line and the reserve were by now following in *Echelon*, and on arrival at the Russian guns the 4th and 8th joined the remnants of the 13th and 17th, while the 11th Hussars on the left swept past the guns to find, at a short distance in front of them, the same Hussars and Cossacks of Rijoff's Brigade

that had been worsted by the Heavy Brigade. Already shaken by their previous rough handling, these found the sight of their own artillery teams bolting away too much for them, and the whole mass turned tail and ran. They were closely pursued by the 11th who, now only about 80 men strong, appear to have been acting on their own, while the 4th and the 8th were still some distance behind. After joining the remnants of the first line, covering their withdrawal, and advancing a short distance beyond the guns, the 4th and 8th themselves withdrew, riding back through heavy enemy fire and attacks by Russian lancers from either flank. The 11th Hussars, having reached the very end of the valley, came face to face with the now rallying Russian cavalry, and held them at bay for several minutes until the appearance of the Russian lancers in their rear forced them to turn and make for home.

All order was lost, and the horrified spectators on the Sapoune Heights saw only a few stragglers emerging from the smoke-filled valley below them; but, although apparently almost wiped out, the final count revealed that nearly 400 of the 660 men involved had survived 'Whether the charge was justified', wrote Lt. Col. Maude in 1903, '. . . may remain open to question; but the fact remains, that an overwhelming force of artillery and infantry fire failed altogether to stop or check the rush of

Charge of the Light Cavalry Brigade, 25th Octr 1854; *original watercolour sketch by William Simpson later published as a lithograph in the series* Seat of War in the East. *(National Army Museum)*

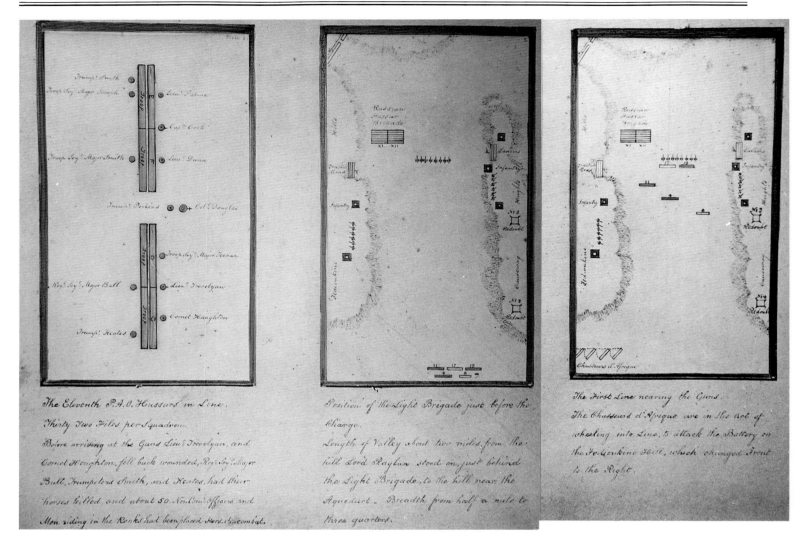

The Eleventh P.A.O. Hussars in Line.

Thirty Two Files per Squadron.

Before arriving at the Guns Lieut. Trevelyan, and Cornet Houghton, fell back wounded, Regt. Sejt. Major Bull, Trumpeters Smith, and Keates, had their horses killed, and about 50 Non Com. Officers and Men riding in the Ranks had been placed Hors de combat.

Position of the Light Brigade just before the Charge.

Length of Valley about two miles from the hill Lord Raglan stood on, just behind the Light Brigade, to the hill near the Aqueduct. Breadth from half a mile to three quarters.

The First Line nearing the Guns.

The Chasseurs d'Afrique are in the act of wheeling into Line, to attack the Battery on the Fedioukine Hill, which changed Front to the Right.

View down the North Valley in the direction taken by the charge of the Light Brigade, showing Kamara in the right middle distance and the Traktir bridge in the left middle distance. The only known photograph of the North Valley, it is taken from Colonel Klembowski's volume of views of the Crimea published in Russia in 1904. (Mollo Collection)

Plan of the Charge of the Light Brigade drawn by Sergeant-Major G.L.Smith, 11th Hussars. (Royal Hussars)

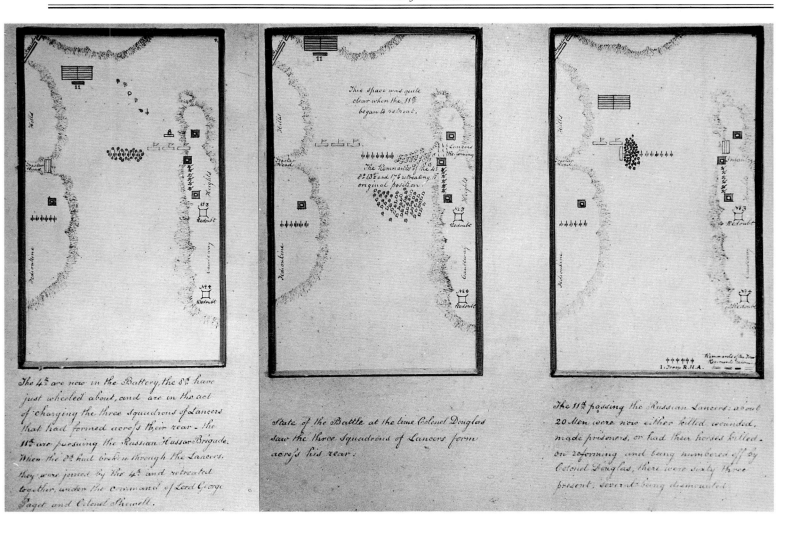

The 4th are now in the Battery, the 8th have just wheeled about, and are in the act of charging the three squadrons of Lancers that had formed across their rear. The 11th are pursuing the Russian Hussar Brigade. When the 8th had broken through the Lancers, they were joined by the 4th and retreated together, under the command of Lord George Paget and Colonel Shewell.

State of the Battle at the time Colonel Douglas saw the three Squadrons of Lancers form across his rear.

The 11th passing the Russian Lancers: about 20 Men were now either killed, wounded, made prisoners, or had their horses killed. On reforming and being numbered off by Colonel Douglas, there were sixty three present, several being dismounted.

disciplined cavalry well led. Neither were our losses very serious until the retreat began; and most of these might have been avoided, had it been possible to support the charge properly'.

The Heavy Brigade had in fact advanced on the right in support of the charge, with Lord Lucan and his staff acting as a connecting link between the two brigades, as far down the valley as No.3 Redoubt. At this point the crossfire was so severe that Lucan halted and then withdrew the Heavy Brigade. After two successive *Echelon* movements the Brigade halted in its new position, 'sufficiently advanced to protect the retreat of the Light Brigade'. The losses sustained by the Heavy Brigade during this phase of the battle, and in particular by the Greys and Royals in the first line, far exceeded those incurred during its earlier charge.

The parade strength of the Light Brigade on the 25th, and the casualties that were subsequently incurred, seem to differ in every account. Possibly the most reliable are those given in *From Corunna to Sevastopol*, which were 'carefully compiled from the Regimental Records, and verified as far as possible by some of the survivors'. They are as follows:—

Regt	Went into Action	Returned	Losses Officers & Men	Losses Horses
4LD	126	81	45	61
8H	115	67	48	46
11H	142	79	63	72
13LD	128	72	56	84
17L	147	72	75	99
	658	371	287	362

Sergeant-Major Loy Smith, basing his figures on the official returns of 26 October signed by the Adjutant-General, gives a total of 676 all ranks, with 277 losses of officers and men, and 335 horses. The losses among the horses were almost certainly higher as many were put down later. According to one source 113 were all that were left, and the majority of these were to die from exposure and starvation during the rigours of the following winter.

Finally, it is interesting to note from the above figures that the two regiments in the first line and the 11th Hussars in the second line had the most casualties, which suggests that the disabling of the Cossack Horse Artillery Battery in the North Valley reduced quite considerably the amount of fire inflicted on the two regiments in the reserve line.

Clothing and Accoutrements

Introduction

In the years following the defeat of Napoleon at Waterloo British cavalry uniform had reached a high point of absurdity and richness, largely through the influence of George IV, who encouraged every sort of sartorial excess. With the accession of William IV, however, the dress of the army became slightly simpler, although his desire to clothe in red those units who had worn blue, mainly light cavalry, put them to considerable expense. In 1840, three years after the accession of Queen Victoria, the same regiments, with the exception of the 16th Lancers, changed back to their former blue uniforms, again no doubt at considerable expense. Uniform clothing was tight and constricting, but towards the end of the 1840s there was a move towards a looser cut in imitation of civilian fashion, which culminated in new uniforms for the whole army. Although these were approved before the outbreak of the Crimean War they were not issued until 1856. The moving force behind these reforms, which introduced the tunic to the British army, was the Prince Consort, who has been credited with the idea of the German-style metal helmet authorised for the Household Cavalry in 1842, and the regiments of Dragoon Guards and Dragoons in 1849.

**The Regulation and Provision
of Clothing and Equipment**

Officers—The details of the dress and accoutrements of Officers were laid down in *Dress Regulations* which were published from time to time, and which were amended, as required, by *Circular Memoranda* issued by Horse Guards. In 1854 the Dress Regulations in force were those of 1846.

Subject to the requirements of the Regulations, the details of helmet and shako plates, pouch, sabretache, and shabraque ornamentation, buttons, waist-belt plates, and other similar ornaments were a matter for the regiments themselves.

Officers were responsible for the ordering and purchase of their own uniforms and accoutrements, and to ensure adherence to the Regulations the various military tailors maintained pattern books showing the relevant details.

Other Ranks—No dress regulations were issued for Other Ranks; instead, the design, cut, and construction of each item of clothing and equipment were approved by the Consolidated Board of General Officers, and sealed patterns of the items were deposited at the Office of Military Boards, for the guidance of clothiers and manufacturers. Regiments were informed of any changes through *Memoranda* issued by Horse Guards.

When completed the new clothing was sent to cavalry regiments tailored to each individual man, and accompanied by a sealed pattern of each article, so that Commanding Officers could judge whether the articles had been made up correctly.

The provision of the soldier's complete kit, which was divided into **Clothing, Necessaries,** and **Accoutrements,** was governed by the *Royal Warrant and Regulations regarding Army Services,* published at the War Office on 1 July 1848. This specified the articles to be provided, and how often; who was to pay for them; and the sums of money, known as 'off-reckonings', allowed to Colonels of regiments for equipping their men. The details varied according to where a regiment was stationed, and only such extracts as are applicable to regiments ordered to the East are given here.

Clothing

This was to be provided at the expense of the respective Colonels, when they were entitled to off-reckonings; and of the public when the Colonels were not so entitled. The items to be provided and the length of time which they were expected to last were as follows:—

DRAGOON GUARDS AND DRAGOONS | *Replacement*
Metal helmet complete with plume. | Once every four years.
1 Dress Jacket. ⎫
1 Undress Jacket. ⎬ Once every two years.
1 Pair of Overalls. ⎭

LIGHT DRAGOONS
Felt Cap (shako) complete with plume. | Once every four years.
1 Dress Jacket. ⎫
1 Undress Jacket. ⎪
1 Pair of Overalls. ⎬ Once every two years.
1 Cap Line. ⎪
1 Cap Case. ⎭

HUSSARS
Fur Cap complete with plume. | Once every four years.
1 Dress Jacket. ⎫
1 Pelisse. ⎪
1 Undress Jacket. ⎬ Once every two years.
1 Pair of Overalls. ⎪
1 Cap Line. ⎪
1 Cap Case. ⎭

LANCERS
Lance Cap complete with plume. | Once every four years.
1 Dress Jacket. ⎫
1 Undress Jacket. ⎪
1 Pair of Overalls. ⎬ Once every two years.
1 Cap Line. ⎪
1 Cap Case. ⎭

Necessaries

These were to be provided and kept up at the expense of the soldier.

All Cavalry

2 Prs. Long Web Drawers.	2 Towels.
1 Pr. Gauntlets.	1 Clothes Brush.
1 Pr. Gloves.	2 Shoe Brushes.
1 Pr. Boots.	1 Hair Comb.
1 Pr. Highlows.	1 Razor.
1 Pr. Spurs.	1 Shaving Brush.
1 Forage Cap and Strap.	1 Knife and Fork.
1 Girdle or Sash.	1 Spoon.
2 Flannel Waistcoats.	1 Button Stick.
1 Pr. Cloth Overalls.	1 Brass Brush.
1 Pr. Braces.	1 Tin Bottle for Oil.
3 Shirts.	1 Tin of Blacking.
1 Stock & Clasp.	1 Pipe-Clay Sponge.
3 Prs. Worsted Hose.	1 Holdall.
1 Mess Tin and Cover, when ordered for Service.	

Accoutrements and Appointments

These were to be provided at the expense of the Colonel. All items were expected to last 12 years, except where otherwise indicated. All items were to be marked with the number or name of the Regiment, the Troop letter, and the year in which each was issued. The items concerned were as follows:—

1 Sword Knot.	18 years.
1 Waistbelt, with Plate, Catch and Hook.	18 years.
1 Long Sword Carriage with Billet.	
1 Short Sword Carriage with Billet.	
1 Pouch (10 Rounds).	18 Years.
1 Pouchbelt, Buckle, Tip, and Slide.	18 Years.
1 Sabretach with Straps. (Hussars only)	
1 Sword Scabbard.	
1 Pocket for Percussion Caps (12 Caps).	
1 Axe with Case and Belt (Farriers).	20 Years.
1 Cloak.	10 Years.

Camp Equipage

This covered articles not normally part of the soldier's accoutrements, but which were necessary for service in the field:—

Haversacks.	Cooking Pots.
Water Canteens.	Billhooks.
Blankets.	

Troops destined for the Crimea received their haversacks before embarkation, but were not issued with the other items until their arrival in the East.

Orders of Dress

The different items of clothing to be worn, and equipment to be carried on different occasions, were sometimes listed in *Regimental Standing Orders*; and it is possible, by taking these together, to get a good idea of how all ranks were dressed for their various duties.

Officers, Mounted:

Review Order—Full dress, epaulettes, gold appointments, sheepskin and housing (5 DG 1842). Full dress, steel spurs, leopard skin, shabraque, cloak and collar chain (16L 1852).

Marching Order—Oilskin undress lance cap, undress lines, stable jacket, gauntlets, pouch-belt, undress sword-belt, sheepskin, cloak and collar chain (16L).

Light Marching Order—As Marching Order (16L).

Field Day Order—Full dress, shoulder scales, buff belts, cloak and sheepskin (5DG). As Marching Order with the exception of having no cloak, and gloves instead of gauntlets, no collar chain (16L).

Mounted Drill Order—Undress jacket, sword and belt, stripped saddle (5DG). Forage cap, undress jacket, pouch-belt, stripped saddle, gloves (16L).

Riding School Order—As above but without pouch-belt (5DG).

Watering Order, or Horse Parade—Jacket, undress belt and sword (5DG). Undress jacket, cap and sword (16L).

Officers, Dismounted:

Court, Dinner, and Evening Parties—Full dress with epaulettes, full dress appointments, gilt or brass spurs (5DG).

Full Dress—Full dress, sword, and buff belt (5DG). Full dress, yellow metal spurs (16L).

Stable Dress—Jacket, sword and belt (5DG). Blue frock coat, forage cap (16L).

Dress for Town—Jacket in summer; frock in winter (5DG).

Dress Off Duty in Barracks—Frock (5DG).

Other Ranks, Mounted:

Review Order—Full dress, sheepskin, shabraque, cloak and collar chain (16L). Full dress, caps uncased with plume, no baggage, all arms and appointments, gauntlets and collar chains (on off side) (17L 1844).

Marching Order—Full dress lance cap cased, sheepskin, shabraque, cloak collar chain, valise and corn bag (16L). Full dress complete, cap cased, all arms and appointments, valise packed with full kit, gauntlets and collar chains. NB, shabraque turned up on line of march (17L).

Light Marching Order—As above with the exception of having no valise or corn bag (16L).

Field Day Order—Lance cap cased, cap-lines, undress jacket, gloves, sheepskin (16L). Undress, cap cased, gauntlets, cloaks and all arms, collar chains (17L).

Drill Order—Forage cap, undress jacket, pouch-belt, gloves, stripped saddle (16L). Undress and all arms (17L).

Riding School Order—As above but without pouch-belt (16L).

Watering Order—As above, mounted on blanket, with snaffle, without arms, bit, or saddle (16L). Undress, blanket only, with web surcingle, bridoon and bridle (17L).

Other Ranks, Dismounted:

Stable Dress—As Riding School Order but without spurs or straps (16L).

Full Dress Parade (on foot)—Full dress (16L).

Dragoon Guards and Heavy Dragoons

The Heavy Brigade consisted of two Regiments of Dragoon Guards, the 4th and 5th, and three Regiments of Dragoons, the 1st Royal, 2nd Royal North British, and 6th Inniskilling. These last three were celebrated in having formed the Union Brigade at Waterloo, where the Royals and the Scots Greys both captured French Eagles.

The Royals were raised in 1661 as the Tangier Troop of Horse, and became the 1st Dragoons in 1684. The Scots Greys were raised in 1672 on the outbreak of the war with Holland. The 4th and 5th Dragoon Guards dated from the period of increase in the army in 1685 during the reign of James II, with the 6th Dragoons following in 1689, as a result of the Irish War. The 4th and 5th were given precedence, as regiments of Horse, over the Dragoons, who were then considered as mounted infantry rather than cavalry. The regiments of Horse were designated Dragoon Guards in 1788.

Although the uniform of the army changed little between 1829 and 1855, that of the Heavy Cavalry underwent considerable alteration with the introduction of a new pattern coatee in 1847, and a new helmet in 1849.

Dragoon Guards could be distinguished from Dragoons (from 1855) by having gilt or brass helmets, as opposed to silver or white metal, as ordered for the latter in that year; and by having velvet instead of cloth facings. In addition the Scots Greys could always be readily identified by their bearskin grenadier caps. Other methods of distinguishing between the regiments were:—

1. The facing colour of the collar, cuffs, and skirt turn-backs of the coatees:—
   4th DG, 1st RD, and 2nd RNBD — dark blue.
   5th DG — dark green.
   6th D — yellow.

2. Regimental pattern sabretaches and shabraques, embroidered with individual regimental devices and distinctions.

3. Regimental pattern pouch and pouch-belts, embroidered with individual regimental devices and distinctions.

4. Regimental pattern helmet plates.

5. Epaulettes, shoulder scales, waist-belt plates, and buttons, bearing the regimental number and other special devices.

Officers' Dress Regulations reproduced from 'Dress Regulations for the Army 1846':

DRAGOON GUARDS

AND

HEAVY DRAGOONS.

DRESS

Coat—scarlet: collar, cuffs, and turnbacks of regimental facings, which in Dragoon Guards are to be of velvet, in Heavy Dragoons of cloth;— single-breasted, with nine uniform buttons in front; two loops on each end of the collar; turnbacks laced; embroidered skirt ornaments. The Dragoon Guards have four loops on the sleeve, placed two and two; the Heavy Dragoons three at equal distances. The loops of the Dragoon Guards are to be of gold embroidery; those of the Heavy Dragoons of gold lace. The entire loop in each case not to exceed one inch and three quarters in breadth and the lace on the turnbacks half that breadth.

Epaulettes—gold bullion, boxed, with strap and crescent embroidered in gold, on velvet in the Dragoon Guards and on cloth in the Heavy Dragoons, of the colour of the regimental facings. The regimental badge of each regiment embroidered in silver within the crescent.

Helmet*—gilt brass, with regimental ornaments and devices in front, and an ornamented crest (three inches and a half deep) in which is inserted a mane of black horse-hair (two feet ten inches long) flowing loose behind and terminating in front in a thistle-shaped brush, confined by a gold embroidered boss; gilt brass scales.

* The Second, or Royal North British Dragoons, have permission to wear a bearskin cap with a white hackle feather, nine inches long according to regimental pattern.

(continued on page 36)

The Dragoon Guards, 1848: 3rd or the Prince of Wales's Dragoon Guards with vignettes of other regiments around the border. Lithograph after Michael Angelo Hayes, no.2 in the series The British Army. (Parker Gallery)

The Dragoons, 1846: the 2nd or Scots Greys, 6th Inniskilling and 1st Royal Dragoons. Lithograph after Michael Angelo Hayes, no.3 in the series The British Army. (National Army Museum)

Officer's jacket, front and back views, 5th Dragoon Guards, 1844-55. (National Army Museum)

An officer of the 4th (Royal Irish) Dragoon Guards, 1854; mounted, in review order. Oil painting by John Ferneley Jr., signed and dated. (Christie's 21 March 1975)

Trousers—dark blue, with a stripe of gold lace, one inch and three quarters wide, down the outward seams.

Boots—ankle.

Spurs—brass.

Sword—steel mounted, with basket hilt.

Scabbard—steel.

Knot—white leather strap, with gold tassel.

Sword-Belt—gold lace, with an edging of velvet, colour of regimental facing, top and bottom; two inches and a half wide, lined with morocco, and fastening in front with a regulation plate same width as belt, and three inches and a quarter long, gilt frosted ground and burnished rim, a silver V.R. in the centre, surmounted by a crown and encircled with oak leaves; the belt to have two sword slings, each one inch and a quarter wide, with gilt buckles and swivels, and three tache-slings, each three quarters of an inch wide, with buckles and loops for rings of tache.

Sash—crimson and gold with pendent tassels.

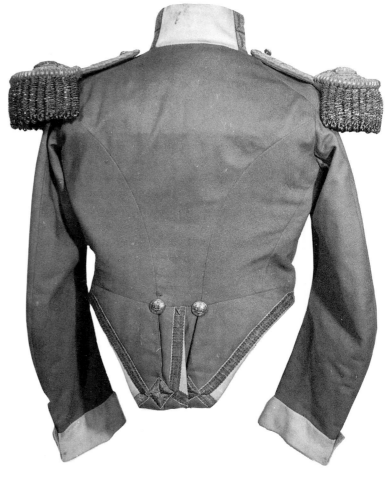

Officer's jacket, front and back views, 6th Inniskilling Dragoons, 1844-55. (Formerly Royal United Service Institution Museum)

Tache—morocco pocket twelve inches and a half deep, ten inches and a half wide at bottom, and eight at top; face, fifteen inches deep, thirteen wide at bottom and nine at top; covered with velvet or cloth, according to regimental facing, and of the same colour, and edged with two and a quarter inch lace, showing a light of the velvet or cloth on the outward edges; a gold embroidered V.R., surmounted by a crown relieved in silver, and encircled with oak leaves; three rings at the top for slings of belt; a morocco case with green baize lining.

Pouch-Belt—gold lace two inches and a half wide; lining and edging to correspond with sword belt; gilt buckle, tip, and slide.

Pouch-Box—morocco leather, colour of regimental facing; back and front covered with velvet or cloth of the same colour; the flap five inches and three quarters wide at top, and six inches and three quarters at bottom; six inches deep; a gold half-inch lace round

the edges, showing a light of the velvet or cloth on the outward edges; a gold embroidered V.R., surmounted by a crown relieved in silver, and encircled with oak leaves.

Stock—black silk.

Gloves—white leather gauntlets.

At Drawing-Rooms, Levees, and in the Evening, instead of the helmet, cocked hat and feather to be worn, viz:—

Hat—cocked, without binding; the fan, or back part, nine inches; the front seven and a half inches; each corner five inches; black ribbons on the two front sides.

Star-Loop—groundwork three ends of dead gold gimp, seven and a half inches long, dead gold star in centre, with studs, diamond and horse-shoe ornaments.

Feather—red and white swan plume, drooping eight inches long.

An officer of the 5th (Princess Charlotte of Wales's) Dragoon Guards, 1853; dismounted, in review order. Watercolour by W.Buckler, signed and dated. (National Army Museum)

An officer of the 1st Royal Dragoons, c1850; mounted, in review order. Oil painting by John Wray Snow, signed and dated. (Sotheby's 25 May 1988)

UNDRESS

Coat
Epaulettes } As for DRESS.
Helmet

Trousers—blue, with a stripe of scarlet cloth, one inch and three quarters wide, down the outward seams.

Spurs—steel.

Gloves—white leather.

Boots
Sword
Scabbard } As for DRESS.
Knot
Sash
Stock

Sword-Belt—white buffalo leather, two inches and a half wide, with gilt mountings; fastening in front with gilt metal regimental plate, three inches long and two and a quarter deep, with silver V.R., crown and laurel; two one-inch wide sword-slings; two half-inch tache-slings, with loop and buckles.

Tache—black patent leather; pocket ten inches deep, nine wide at bottom, and seven and a half at top; plain face 12 inches deep, ten and a half wide at bottom, eight at top; two rings attached to the top for belt-slings.

Pouch-Belt—white buffalo leather; two inches and a half wide, with brass buckle, tip, and slide, and two brass rings, with black patent leather loops attached to them to carry the pouch-box.

Pouch-Box—black patent leather, rounded flap, three inches and a half deep, and six wide, two brass studs to receive the loops in the belt.

Stable-Jacket—scarlet round jacket, single breasted, with small studs quite close down the front, fastening with hooks and eyes; collar two inches and three quarters deep, rounded off in a slope in front, laced round the outer edge, and edged with gold gimp chain along the collar seam; pointed cuffs, five inches deep at point,

laced round the top; the collar, cuffs, and edging at the bottom of jacket, of the regimental facing; the jacket laced all round with gold lace, forming bull's-eye ornaments at the hips, which shew a light of the regimental facing; the whole of the lace three quarters of an inch wide, and the same for officers of all ranks. Shoulder cords of twisted gold gimp chain (same as on the collar), with small regimental buttons.

Frock-Coat—blue; single-breasted, with six loops in front, and four rows of olivets; stand-up collar, with figured pattern; pointed cuff, with ornamental figure, extending altogether four inches up the arm.

Forage Cap—blue cloth, encircled by a gold-lace band, one inch and three quarters wide; a figure in gold Russia braid at the top; black patent leather peak embroidered; black patent leather chin-strap.

Cloak—scarlet, lined with white shalloon.

REGIMENTAL STAFF.

The Adjutant to wear the uniform of his rank.

The Paymaster, Quarter-Master, Surgeon, Assistant-Surgeon, and Veterinary Surgeon, to wear the same uniform as the other officers, except that they wear no sash, and instead of the helmet a cocked hat.

The Paymaster and Quarter-Master wear the regimental loops and tassels. The Quarter-Master, only, wears a feather. The Surgeon, Assistant-Surgeon, and Veterinary Surgeon, wear a black loop and tassels, but no feather.

An officer of the 2nd Dragoons (Royal Scots Greys), 1852; mounted, in review order. Oil painting by T.Bretland, signed and dated. (Parker Gallery)

Officer's undress sabretache, 4th Dragoon Guards, c1850-55. (Formerly RUSI Museum)

Officer's undress sabretache, 1st Royal Dragoons, c1850-55. (Formerly RUSI Museum)

Officers of the 4th Dragoon Guards entertaining French officers in their camp, spring 1855. Photograph by Roger Fenton. (Army Museums Ogilby Trust)

Additional items not fully described in the Dress Regulations:

Sabretaches and Pouches—A *Circular Memorandum*, dated 17 April 1854, announcing changes in the uniform of the Army, specified that ' . . . the sabretache will not be worn except in Hussar regiments . . . '. Although these changes did not take effect until the following year, the Heavy Cavalry regiments left their sabretaches behind when they sailed for the East.

The basic design described in the Regulations was followed reasonably closely by the 5th Dragoon Guards, and the Scots Greys; but other regiments had their own, more distinctive patterns, the Royals, in particular, having their battle honours embroidered over the lace at the top and bottom of the sabretache. The colour details of the sabretaches and pouches illustrated here are as follows:—

4TH DRAGOON GUARDS—Dark blue velvet face; gold lace and embroidery; silver star of the Order of St Patrick, with a red cross in the centre. 15 inches high, nine and a half inches wide at the top, and 12½ inches wide at the bottom.

5TH DRAGOON GUARDS—Green velvet face; gold lace and embroidery.

Officer's undress sabretache, 6th Inniskilling Dragoons, c1850-55. (Parker Gallery)

Major Burton, 5th Dragoon Guards, spring 1855; mounted, in marching order. Photograph by Roger Fenton. (5th Royal Inniskilling Dragoon Guards)

1ST ROYAL DRAGOONS—Dark blue cloth face; gold lace and embroidery; crimson velvet lining to crown; silver embroidered battle honours.

2ND R.N.B. DRAGOONS—Dark blue cloth face; gold lace and embroidery; crimson velvet lining to crown; crimson scroll.

6TH DRAGOONS—White cloth in centre; red cloth round edge; gold lace and embroidery; silver castle and honour scroll. 13 inches high, eight and a half inches wide at the top, 11¼ inches wide at the base.

Examples of two undress sabretaches are illustrated. These adhere fairly closely to the Regulations, except that both have gilt regimental badges instead of the 'plain face' required by the Regulations.

Buttons

4TH DRAGOON GUARDS—Incised star of St. Patrick, with the circle inscribed RIDG and QUIS SEPERABIT.

5TH DRAGOON GUARDS—V above DG in relief, on a ribbed ground, within a Crowned Garter inscribed VESTIGIA NULLA RETRORSUM.

1ST ROYAL DRAGOONS—The Lion of England, without a Crown, within a Crowned Garter inscribed ROYAL DRAGOONS.

2ND R.N.B. DRAGOONS—Within a scalloped rim a French Eagle, with WATERLOO inscribed on the base, all above the letters RNBD.

6TH DRAGOONS—Within a scalloped rim, the Castle of Inniskilling above the number VI.

Officer's helmet, 4th Dragoon Guards, 1847-73. (Butler Collection)

Officer's helmet, back view, 5th Dragoon Guards, 1847-73. (National Army Museum)

Uniform changes between 1846 and 1854

There were two major changes in Heavy Cavalry uniform between the publication of the *1846 Dress Regulations* and the Crimean War. In 1847 the coatee was simplified and shortened to a jacket style; and two years later a new pattern helmet was introduced. The announcement of the new pattern jacket was given in a *Circular Memorandum* for Commanding Officers of Heavy Cavalry, dated 3 December 1847: 'Some alterations having been authorised to be made in the coatee of the regiments of heavy cavalry, an approved pattern showing the alterations has been sealed and deposited. The officers are to be dressed precisely like the men as to pattern, and the coatee is to be entirely divested of padding and stuffing'.

The second sentence showed the usual optimism in such matters on the part of Horse Guards, but, while the officers' jacket was never 'precisely like' the mens', it was markedly simpler than the previous pattern. The illustrated example of that of the 6th Dragoons shows the main changes, which consisted in the removal of all but one of the lace chevrons on the lower sleeve, and the shortening of the coat-tails.

The new metal helmet was authorised by a *Circular Memorandum*, dated 23 October 1849. It was similar to, but slightly simpler than the 'Albert' helmet adopted by the Household Cavalry in 1842, which was the first helmet of *pickelhaube* style adopted by the British Army. The helmet was described in detail in the 1857 *Dress Regulations*:—

Col. White's helmet after Balaclava; 6th Inniskilling Dragoons, 1847-73. (5th Royal Inniskilling Dragoon Guards)

Helmet—For the seven regiments of Dragoon Guards, gilt brass, the front and back peaks ornamented with a scroll wreath; a band of the same character round the bottom and up the back of the helmet; front ornamented within a shield, a diamond cut silver star, upon which is a garter bearing the title of the regiment, and encircling the cypher VR; above the shield a crown, and below it, a wreath of olive and oak extending upwards. A chin-strap of plain chain lined with black leather, fastening on each side to a rose ornament. On top of the helmet a socket for a plume. (For the 1st or Royal Dragoons, and the 6th or Inniskilling, a helmet of white metal of the same pattern, with gilt ornaments, was introduced in 1855.)

Plume—Black horse hair with a rose at the top, standing five inches above the top of the helmet. Coloured plumes were in fact specified, but until 1857 all regiments wore black.

Forage Cap—In 1853 a new pattern of forage cap was approved for all cavalry regiments. This replaced the pattern with the wide soft crown with the pill-box cap which was to remain in use until after 1900.

2nd Dragoons (Royal Scots Greys), c1854; two sergeants dismounted, in review order, front and back views. Watercolour by Lt.Col.Count Pajol. (Brunon Collection)

Rank and File

Jacket—Red; collar, cuffs, and turnbacks of regimental facing colour; single-breasted, with nine pewter regimental buttons in front; two yellow worsted lace loops on each end of the collar; a single V shaped lace loop, with a button in the centre, on each cuff. In the Dragoon Guards the collar and cuff loops were pointed and ended in a tassel; in the Dragoons they were square-ended. Turn-backs laced; skirt ornaments a diamond of lace with a button in the centre. Sergeant-Majors had gold lace in place of yellow worsted.

Shoulder-scales—Brass, with seven plain scales, and a raised crescent, attached by means of a button, and a brass bridge sewn to the shoulder of the jacket.

Badges of Rank—

Regimental Sergeant-Majors to wear:	Four chevrons and a crown above.
Troop Sergeant-Majors to wear:	Three chevrons and a crown above.
Other Sergeants to wear:	Three chevrons only.
Corporals to wear:	Two chevrons only.

The chevrons were worn on the lower right arm above the cuff by Regimental Sergeant-Majors, with the points facing upwards, and on the upper right arm, with the points facing downwards, by the remainder. The chevrons of Sergeant-Majors and Sergeants were made of gold lace, and those of Corporals of yellow worsted lace; all were backed on cloth of the facing colour, and sewn with the extremities extending to within half an inch of the sleeve seams.

Good Conduct Badges—Chevrons of yellow worsted lace, edged with the regimental facing colour, worn with the points up above the right cuff.

Trumpeters—The Trumpeters of the 4th Dragoon Guards, and the 1st and 6th Dragoons, wore red helmet plumes and gold aiguilettes on the right shoulder. Those of the Scots Greys wore red plumes in their bearskin caps, and, in 1838, short gold fringes on their shoulder-scales. The Trumpeters of the 1st Dragoons also wore a badge of crossed trumpets, embroidered in yellow worsted on a blue backing, which was worn on the right upper-arm. For Trumpet-Majors it was in gold and worn between the crown and the chevrons.

Farriers—Badges, consisting of a horseshoe embroidered in yellow worsted (gold for Farrier-Majors) on a backing of the facing colour, were worn on the right upper arm of the jacket.

Helmet—As Officers, but made of brass in the Dragoon Guards, and (from 1855) white metal in the Dragoons.

The 5th Dragoon Guards in stable dress watering horses, Melton Mowbray, 1852. Oil painting by John Ferneley Jr., signed and dated. (Army Museums Ogilby Trust)

Capt. White with men of his troop, 6th Inniskilling Dragoons. 1848. Watercolour by H.de Daubrawa. (Parker Gallery)

1st Royal Dragoons, details of other ranks' uniform, accoutrements and saddlery, c1854. Pencil drawing by General Vanson. (Musée de l'Armée)

Bearskin Cap—Worn by the 2nd R.N.B. Dragoons only; black fur with a white hackle feather, nine inches long, on the left side, secured by a brass grenade; a white metal White Horse of Hanover in the centre back of the cap; brass chin chain mounted on black leather.

Trousers—Blue cloth, with a single yellow cloth stripe one and three quarters inches wide down each outside seam (gold lace for Sergeant-Majors).

Boots—Ankle.

Spurs—Steel.

Stock—Black leather.

Gloves—White buff leather gauntlets.

Undress

Forage Cap—Blue cloth; with a yellow cloth band two inches deep, except in the 2nd R.N.B. Dragoons, who had a blue band with white vandyked lacing round the band; yellow worsted button on top (a red *Tourie* for the 2nd Dragoons); black leather chin-strap with adjusting buckle.

Stable-Jacket—Red; single-breasted, with nine pewter regimental buttons in front; plain collar and pointed cuffs in the regimental facing colour; yellow cord shoulder-straps with a regimental button. Sergeant-Majors had gold lace edging to the collar and cuffs, and gold cord shoulder-straps. Farriers wore blue stable-jackets with blue collars and cuffs.

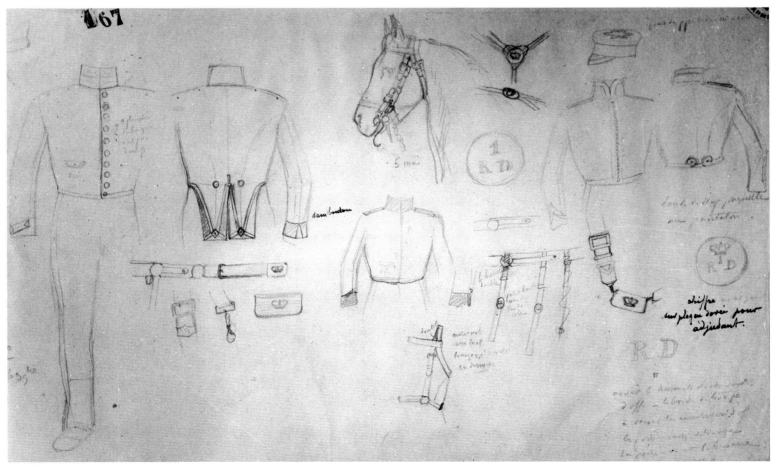

Light Dragoons

Two of the regiments composing the Light Brigade, the 4th and the 13th, were still clothed and equipped as Light Dragoons, a form of cavalry which first appeared in the British Army in the middle of the 18th century as Light Troops in Dragoon Regiments. The first regiment of Light Dragoons, later numbered the 15th, was raised in 1759, and over the next 25 years new regiments were formed, and several existing Dragoon regiments were converted to Light Dragoons, among them the 11th and 13th, in 1783. The last two Dragoon regiments to be made 'Light' were the 3rd and 4th, in 1818. By then, however, Light Dragoons were themselves being converted into Hussars and Lancers, so that by 1854 only four regiments of Light Dragoons remained: the 3rd, 4th, 13th and 14th, which all became Hussars in 1860-61.

The uniform worn by the Light Dragoons in 1854 dated from the changes of 1829-30. Since the 1780s it had been the custom to clothe the Heavy Cavalry in red, and the Light Cavalry in blue. William IV had altered this so that the entire cavalry was dressed in red, but soon after his death in 1837 the Light Cavalry reverted to their former blue. In 1844 the elaborate bell-topped shako was replaced ·by a smaller and simpler version. With these exceptions the uniform described in the 1846 *Dress Regulations* changed little between 1829 and 1855.

The different regiments of Light Dragoons could be distinguished in the following ways:—

1. The facing colour on the collar, cuffs, and skirt turn-backs of the jacket:—

    3rd, 4th, and 14th Light Dragoons — red.
    13th Light Dragoons — buff (in practice white).

2. Regimental pattern sabretaches and shabraques, embroidered with individual regimental distinctions.

3. Pouches and pouch-belts; these were standard except that the lace of the belt had a quarter-inch 'train', or centre stripe in the facing colour. The same applied to the sword-belts and sabretache slings.

4. Regimental pattern shako plates and buttons bearing the regimental number and other special devices.

Officers' Dress Regulations reproduced from 'Dress Regulations for the Army 1846':

LIGHT DRAGOONS
DRESS.

Jacket—blue; double breasted, two rows of buttons, eight in each row, the distance between the rows two inches and a half at top, one and a half at bottom; collar, cuffs, and turnbacks, colour of regimental facings; gold bullion back-pieces; plaited skirts, with three buttons on each side; the collar, cuffs, and sleeves edged with five-eighth inch gold basket braid, and ornamented with small gold Russia braid.

Epaulettes—with plain lace straps, and gold double bullion crescent, gold bullion two inches and a half deep.

Chaco (sic)—black beaver, seven inches deep in front, eight inches at back, and eight inches diameter at top; patent leather sunk top, bound with gold oak-leaf lace, an inch and three quarters wide; gilt and silver cross plate, with regimental badges; patent leather peak, embroidered with gold to the width of one inch; gilt chain, fastening at sides with rose-pattern ornaments.

Cap-Line—gold cord with olive ends, worn twice round the cap, and crossing at the back.

Plume—white swan feathers, five inches on the mount, the outer drooping feathers fourteen inches long. In India white horse-hair of the same dimensions. Gilt socket.

Trousers—dark blue, with two stripes down each outward seam, of gold lace, three quarters of an inch wide, leaving a light between.

Boots—ankle.

Spurs—yellow metal.

Sabre—steel mounted, half-basket hilt, with two fluted bars on the outside, black fish-skin gripe (sic) bound with silver wire; the blade very little curved, thirty-five inches and a half long, and one inch and a quarter wide, with a round back, terminating within eleven inches of the point.

The Light Dragoons, 1846: 4th Regiment of Light Dragoons with vignettes of other regiments around the border. Lithograph after Michael Angelo Hayes, no.4 in the series The British Army. *(Parker Gallery)*

Capt. J. Anstruther Thomson, 13th Light Dragoons, in marching order, c1854. Watercolour by Michael Angelo Hayes. (National Army Museum)

Scabbard—steel, with large shoe at the bottom, solid band and rings, a trumpet-formed mouth.

Knot—gold cord, with acorn end.

Girdle—gold lace, three inches wide, with two three-eighth crimson silk stripes; red morocco lining; fastening underneath with a leather strap and buckle, and externally with three gold cord loops and embroidered olivets.

Waist-Belt—gold lace one inch and a quarter wide, with a quarter-inch silk stripe up the centre; morocco lining and edging, fastening in front with a snake-ornament; two large and one smaller gilt rings, through which hang three slings of inch silk and gold vellum lace, with buckles and straps, by which the tache is suspended, and two slings of one inch and a quarter wide gold and silk lace, with swivels for rings of scabbard; the silk stripes, and morocco lining and edging, of the colour of facings.

Sabre-Tache—purple leather pocket, twelve and a half inches deep, ten inches and a half wide at bottom, eight inches at top; blue cloth face, fourteen inches deep, fourteen inches wide at bottom, eight inches and a half at top; edged round with two inch and a quarter gold lace, showing a blue edge; embroidered V.R. in the centre, surmounted by a crown; three rings at top for slings of belt; a morocco case.

Pouch-Belt—gold lace, two inches wide, with half-inch silk stripe, lining, and edging to correspond with waist-belt; silver engraved plates with chains and pickers, buckle, tip, and slide; attached to pouch-box with silver buckles and rings.

Pouch-Box—Black leather, a gold embroidered edging round the top; solid silver flap, seven inches and a half wide, two inches and three quarters deep; engraving round the edges; gilt raised V.R., surmounted by a crown, in the centre; on each side silver staple ornaments for rings of belt.

Stock—black silk.

Gloves—white leather.

UNDRESS.

Trousers—blue, with two stripes down each outward seam, of scarlet cloth, three quarters of an inch wide, leaving a light between*.

* In the 13th Light Dragoons the stripes are buff, according to the regimental facings.

Spurs—steel, with sharp rowels.

Waist-Belt—black patent leather, two inches wide, with gilt lion's head mounting, fastening in front with a snake-ornament; two large and one smaller gilt rings, through which hang three tache-slings half an inch wide, fastening with buckles and straps to rings of sabre-tache, and two sword-slings, each one inch wide, with swivels for rings of scabbard.

Sabre-Tache—plain black patent leather, nine inches and a half wide at top, nine at bottom; face, twelve inches deep; eight inches wide at top, ten and a half at bottom; three gilt rings at top for slings of belt.

Black oilskin foul weather cap for Light Dragoons, 1844- 1855. (Queen's Royal Irish Hussars)

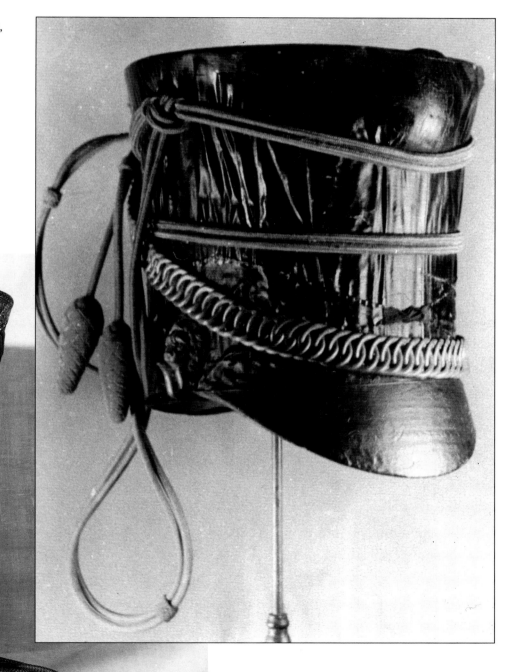

Officer's shako, 4th Light Dragoons, 1844-55. (McAlpine Collection)

Pouch-Belt—plain white buffalo leather, two inches wide, attached to pouch-box.

Pouch-Box—black patent leather, rounded top; flap six inches and a half wide, four and a half deep.

Jacket
Epaulettes
Chaco, with oiled-silk cover
Boots
Sabre } As in DRESS.
Scabbard
Knot
Stock
Gloves

Stable-Jacket—blue round jacket, single-breasted, with small studs quite close down the front; fastening with hooks and eyes; Prussian collar three inches deep, laced round outward edge; pointed cuff four inches deep at point, laced round the top; collar, cuffs, and edging round the bottom of jacket, of the regimental facing; the jacket trimmed all round with gold lace. Field Officers to wear lace one inch and a half wide; other Officers, lace one inch wide.

Officer's jacket, front and back views, 4th Light Dragoons, 1840-55. (Queen's Royal Irish Hussars)

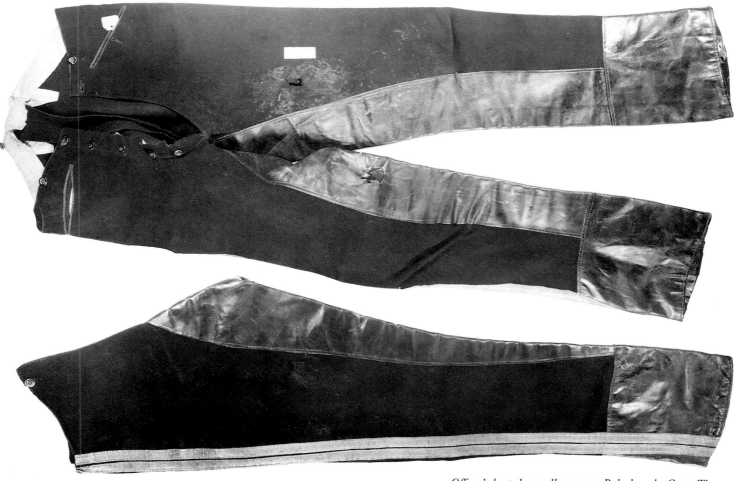

Officer's booted overalls worn at Balaclava by Capt. Thomas Hutton, 4th Light Dragoons. (Queen's Royal Irish Hussars)

Shoulder-Straps—gold cord and button.

Forage-Cap—blue cloth, with welts and plaits; gold oak-leaf band one inch and three quarters wide; gold basket button at top; black patent leather peak embroidered, chin-strap, and oil- skin cover.

Frock-Coat—blue; single-breasted, with six loops in front, and four rows of olivets; stand-up collar with figured pattern, pointed cuff, with ornamental figure, extending altogether four inches up the arm.

Cloak—blue cloth, lined with scarlet; collar of regimental facing.

DRESS OF REGIMENTAL STAFF

The Adjutant is to wear the uniform of his rank.

The Dress and Undress of the other Officers of the Regimental Staff are to be the same as those worn by the rest of the Officers, except that the chaco is to be without gold ornaments, and that the girdle is not to be worn.

**Additional items not fully described
in the Dress Regulations:**

Sabretaches—

The *Dress Regulations* do not describe in full the regimental distinctions on the officers' sabretaches. Since these usually included battle honours, the designs changed as often as new ones were awarded. The patterns in use in 1854 were as follows:—

4TH LIGHT DRAGOONS—Blue cloth face; gold lace and embroidery; battle honours embroidered on a red ground. 15 inches high, eight and a half inches wide at the top, and 14 inches wide at the base.

13TH LIGHT DRAGOONS—Blue cloth face; gold lace and embroidery; battle honours and motto embroidered on a crimson velvet ground. Above the cypher PENINSULA, below WATERLOO, and below that the motto VIRET IN AETERNUM.

The sabretache was abolished for regiments of Light Dragoons by the *Circular Memorandum* of 18 April 1854.

Buttons—

4TH LIGHT DRAGOONS—The cypher AR , in relief on a lined ground, within a crowned Garter and Star. The Crown and Star sunk, the Garter in relief, and engraved IV QUEEN'S OWN LD, all in gilt metal.

13TH LIGHT DRAGOONS—XIII above LD engraved within a crowned star of eight points, the design incised; below the Star the motto VIRET IN AETERNUM; above the Star the honours PENINSULA and WATERLOO, all in gilt metal.

Officer's full dress sabretache, 4th Light Dragoons, 1840-1855. (Mollo Collection)

Private's grey overalls, 13th Light Dragoons, 1854. (Formerly RUSI Museum)

Uniform changes between 1846 and 1854

A *War Office Memorandum*, dated 27 November 1849, laid down that yellow stripes should be worn on the overalls of the Light Cavalry in general, with the exception of the 13th Light Dragoons and 17th Lancers, 'which have been specially authorised to have theirs in the colour of the facings', thus replacing the red stripes described in the *Dress Regulations*.

Rank and File

Jacket—Of similar cut to that of the Officers but made of coarser materials. Blue cloth, with collar, pointed cuffs, and turnbacks in the facing colour. The 4th Light Dragoons had yellow worsted braid round the top and front edges of the collar, and around the cuffs. Two rows of eight regimental pewter buttons down the front, three on each skirt pocket flap at the

addition a yellow cord trefoil knot, or 'crowsfoot' above each cuff. It is not clear whether crossed trumpet badges were worn or not.

Girdle—Yellow woven webbing, with two narrow red stripes, fastening at the side with brass toggles and cord loops.

Shako—Similar to that of the Officers, with a one-inch band of yellow worsted lace round the top; white horsehair hanging plume; yellow worsted cap-lines ending in two yellow woven acorns. The plate was made of brass and was similar in design to that of the Officers. The shako was provided with a black oil-cloth cover for wear in marching order.

Trousers—Blue cloth with a double yellow stripe (gold for Sergeant Majors) for the 4th Light Dragoons, and a double white stripe for the 13th Light Dragoons. These stripes were made of cloth, and were each ¾ inch wide, with a narrow 'light' in between. In March 1854 the 13th Light Dragoons was one of four cavalry

back, and two smaller buttons closing each sleeve above the cuff. A small piece of yellow worsted fringe was sewn to the small of the waist at the back. Sergeant-Majors had gold lace in place of yellow worsted.

Shoulder-scales—Brass, with seven plain scales, and a raised crescent, attached by means of a regimental button and a brass bridge sewn to the shoulder of the jacket. A General Order, dated 27 November 1849, stated that a cloth shoulder strap, in the facing colour, was to replace the scales, but this seems to have been ignored.

Badges of Rank—Gold for Sergeant-Majors and Sergeants, and yellow worsted braid for Corporals, each chevron on a backing of the facing colour.

Good Conduct Badges—Yellow worsted braid, each chevron on a backing of the facing colour.

Trumpeters—Piping to the back seams of the jacket in the facing colour; the 4th Light Dragoons having in

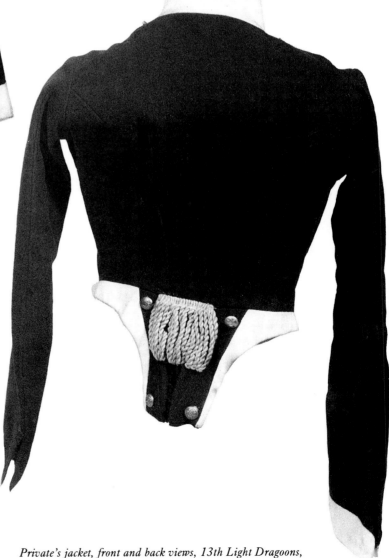

Private's jacket, front and back views, 13th Light Dragoons, 1854. (Formerly RUSI Museum)

regiments issued with grey overalls as an experimental measure, and they embarked for the East wearing them. Like the blue overalls they had the double white stripe down the outside seam.

Boots—Ankle.

Spurs—Steel.

Stock—Black leather.

Undress

Forage-Cap—Blue cloth, with a two-inch cloth band in the regimental facing colour; yellow worsted button on top; black leather chin-strap with adjusting buckle. Trumpeters of the 4th Light Dragoons had a red crown to their caps; and those of the 13th Light Dragoons had a white top, with a blue band and button.

Stable-Jacket—Blue; single-breasted with nine pewter regimental buttons in front; plain collar and pointed cuffs in the regimental facing colour; yellow cord shoulder-strap with a regimental button on each shoulder. Sergeant-Majors had gold lace round collar and cuffs, and gold shoulder-cords. Trumpeters of the 13th Light Dragoons had blue and white mixed braid round the collar and cuffs, forming a trefoil knot above each cuff, and shoulder-straps of the same mixed cord.

Sergeant-Major Short, 4th Light Dragoons, in marching order, c1855. Oil painting, artist unknown. (Queen's Royal Irish Hussars)

COLOUR PLATES A – D

A1: Troop Sergeant-Major, 5th (Princess Charlotte of Wales's) Dragoon Guards; 'Slope Swords'.

This figure wears the order of dress that was worn on the day of the battle. It was similar to No.8 'Patrol Order', as laid down in Cavalry Division Orders for 10 August 1854, but with the dress headdress and jacket in place of the forage-cap and stable-jacket called for in the Orders. The black horse-hair plume has been removed from the brass helmet. The red dress jacket, with its dark green facings and gold embroidered loops and tassels on the collar, is shown without its brass shoulder-scales. The Sergeant-Major's three gold lace chevrons, with their dark green backing, surmounted by a Crown, can be seen on the right upper arm. He wears white buff leather gauntlets, with the strap of the sword-knot looped round the right wrist, and blue 'booted' overalls with a single yellow cloth stripe down the side. The short version of the pouch-belt, without carbine swivel, is worn over the left shoulder, and the straps of the water canteen and haversack over the right shoulder. The brown leather pocket for percussion caps, in this case for use with the pistol, can be seen on the right side of the jacket just above the waist-belt. The 'Slope Swords' position was adopted when 'At Ease' at the halt, or on the march.

A2: Officer, 4th Royal Irish Dragoon Guards; 'Salute – 2nd Movement'.

The helmet, of gilt metal for officers, is worn without its black horse-hair plume; and the dress jacket, with its dark blue velvet facings, and gold embroidered collar loops and tassels, is worn without the gold 'boxed' epaulettes. His gold and crimson sash has its two tassels hanging on the left side. He wears white buff leather gauntlets, and blue booted overalls with a single gold lace stripe down the side. He wears his pouch-belt over the left shoulder, and the strap of his spy-glass case over his right shoulder. His brown leather bridle has gilt scales over the head, and a black horse-hair throat plume, while the collar headstall is lined with red cloth. His black sheepskin is edged with scalloped scarlet cloth; and the shabraque straps, 'spoon' cantle with its brass edging, the rolled scarlet cloak, nearside shoe case, and blanket are all visible. In the second movement of the 'Mounted Officer's Salute' the hand is inclined to the right shoulder, from the 'Recover' (see B2), and the sword is gradually lowered to the right of the thigh until on a line with the knee, the point in the direction of the right foot, and with the edge to the knee.

A3: Corporal, 5th (Princess Charlotte of Wales's) Dragoon Guards; 'Carry Swords'.

This figure, like the previous two, is dressed in modified 'Patrol Order', as worn on the day of the battle. His dress jacket has blue facings, yellow worsted loops and tassels on the collar, and yellow lace edging the skirts, and forming the two chevrons on his right upper arm. He wears white buff leather gauntlets, with the sword-knot looped round the right wrist, and blue booted overalls with a single yellow stripe down the side. The brass buckle, slide, and tip of his pouch-belt, and the black leather pouch, containing twenty rounds, with its brass Star of the Order of St. Patrick, can be clearly seen; as can the way in which the carbine was carried, with its muzzle placed in the bucket, and with the carbine strap fastened round the small of the butt. He wears his canteen and haversack both on the same side, resting on the left hip, at variance with Cavalry Division Orders of 2 June 1854. The spoon cantle of the saddle, projecting through the sheepskin, and the off-side shoe case are clearly seen, as is the steel collar chain used for securing the horse in bivouac. The position 'Carry Swords' was used when 'At Attention' at the halt, or on the march.

B1: Private, 1st (Royal) Dragoons; 'Front Prove Distance'.

The gilt and brass helmets worn in 1854 by two Dragoon regiments, the 1st and 6th, were changed to silver plate and white metal only in 1855. The Private — or 'Dragoon', as he was frequently referred to — is in the modified 'Patrol Order'. His dress jacket has blue facings, with two plain yellow worsted lace loops on the collar, and is without its brass shoulder-scales. He wears white buff leather gauntlets, and blue booted overalls with a single yellow cloth stripe down the side. He wears his canteen strap over his left shoulder, on top of his pouch-belt, and his haversack strap over his right shoulder, passing underneath his pouch-belt, in accordance with Cavalry Division Orders of 2 June 1854. His bridle and horse furniture is similar to that shown in A1 and A3. 'Proving Swords', to the front, and to the right, by extending the sword and sword arm horizontally, was normally done at the beginning of the Sword Exercise to provide sufficient space between the ranks and files, to prevent injury to man and horse, and was carried out at the halt. As the position of 'Front Prove Distance' was almost the same as that taken up on the command 'Charge!', it has been shown here being employed on the move.

B2: Officer, 1st (Royal) Dragoons; 'Recover'.

This officer is in modified 'Patrol Order', without helmet plume and gold epaulettes. His dress jacket has blue cloth facings, gold lace square-ended loops on the collar, and gold lace edging to the turn-backs. He wears his gold and crimson sash under his waist-belt, with the two tassels hanging invisible on the near-side. He has his pouch-belt over his left shoulder, and the strap of his spy-glass case over his right shoulder. He wears white buff leather gauntlets, with the strap of his sword-knot, with its gold plaited acorn, looped over his right wrist; and his blue booted overalls have a single gold lace stripe down the side. His bridle is decorated with gilt scales and bosses, and has a black throat plume; and his black sheepskin is edged with scolloped scarlet cloth. The brass-edged spoon cantle, rolled cloak, and off-side shoe case are also visible. In all these figures the spare end of the stirrup leathers has been rolled up and, together with the heavy buckle, has been positioned just above the stirrup iron. This was in order to provide additional thickness at a point extremely vulnerable to sword cuts. The 'Recover' was also the 1st and 3rd Movements of the 'Mounted Officer's Salute'. The hilt was to be held in front of, and as high as, the under part of the chin, the blade perpendicular, the edge to the left, and the elbow close to the body.

B3: Sergeant, 6th (Inniskilling) Dragoons; 'Cut Seven'.

The Sergeant shown here is in modified 'Patrol Order', without helmet plume and brass shoulder-scales. His dress jacket has a yellow collar, cuffs, and turnbacks, with yellow square-ended worsted lace loops on the collar and cuffs, and yellow worsted lace edging to the turnbacks. His blue booted overalls have a single yellow cloth stripe down the side. In accordance with sketches by the French General Vanson, and Elliot's painting of the charge of the Heavy Brigade, he is shown without gauntlets, and with his water canteen and haversack both resting on his left hip. His saddlery and horse furniture are the same as previously described with the rolled cloak, near-side shoe case, shabraque straps, and brass edged cantle all clearly visible. 'Cut Seven', the last of the seven cuts performed in the Sword Exercise, was to be carried out as follows: 'Raise the arm, with the hand in front, rather above the height of the head, the edge of the sword upwards, and the point lowered to the rear of the right shoulder', then, 'Cut downwards to the front, and remain with the arm extended, the hand in line with the shoulder'.

C1: Officer, 2nd or Royal North British Dragoons; 'First Point'.

The Royal North British Dragoons, or 'Scots Greys' as they were popularly known, were instantly recognisable by means of their black bearskin Grenadier caps, and their grey horses. The officer shown here is in modified No.3 'Marching Order', which according to Elliot's painting was worn on the day of the battle. He has removed the white feather plume from his bearskin cap, and the gold epaulettes from his dress jacket. This last has blue cloth facings, with gold lace loops on the collar, over which is placed a gold embroidered grenade on a blue cloth backing. His sword–knot, looped around his right gauntlet, has a white buff leather strap and a gold plaited acorn. He wears his pouch-belt over his left shoulder, and the strap of his spy-glass case over his right shoulder. His gold and crimson sash is worn under his waist-belt, with the two tassels hanging down on the right side. The Scots Greys landed in the Crimea direct from Constantinople, and were the only regiment to have their valises with them at the time of the battle. These were cylindrical cases of red cloth, the ends being edged round, in the case of the officers, with gold cord, and further decorated with a gold '2' above the letter 'D', also in gold. The first of the three 'Points' in the Sword Exercise consisted in turning the edge of the sword upwards, to the right, and by raising the elbow, and drawing in the wrist just above and in front of the right eye, directing the point of the sword towards the left front.

C2: Private, 2nd or Royal North British Dragoons; 'Cut Four'

This Private, or 'Dragoon', is in No.3 'Marching Order', but without the haynets and cornsack (the latter slung across the seat of the saddle) usually carried on the march. He has dismounted the white plume from his bearskin cap, but the brass grenade socket into which it was fixed can still be seen on the left side. His dress jacket had a blue collar, cuffs and turnbacks, although they are not visible here, with yellow square–ended worsted lace loops, and yellow worsted lace edging to the turnbacks; he has left off the brass shoulder-scales. The brown leather pouch for percussion caps is just visible on the right side of the jacket just above the waist-belt. He wears white buff leather gauntlets, and blue booted overalls with a single yellow cloth stripe down the side. His water canteen and haversack are both slung on the same side, resting on his left hip. His bridlery and horse furniture are as described for the previous figures, except that, like the officer, he has his cylindrical red cloth valise strapped behind his saddle; its circular ends are edged in yellow worsted lace, and have '2' over 'D' in yellow cloth. 'Cut Four' was a backhand cut, starting off with the hand in the hollow of the left shoulder, and then sweeping low on the left side, from rear to front.

C3: Trumpeter, 2nd or Royal North British Dragoons.

Like the previous two Scots Greys figures, the Trumpeter is in 'Marching Order', without haynets and cornsack. Like the others he has dismounted his bearskin plume, which in the case of Trumpeters was red, and his brass shoulder-scales. The small White Horse of Hanover badge, in white metal, can be seen on the back of his bearskin cap. The blue collar and turnbacks of his dress jacket can be seen, together with their yellow worsted lace decoration. An unusual feature, shown by Vanson in one of his sketches, is the fact that he is wearing the long pouch-belt for use with the carbine, but shorn of its carbine swivel and clip. The black leather pouch with its brass Napoleonic Eagle badge, worn in memory of Waterloo, is clearly visible. He is sounding a call on his brass and copper bugle, which was used for 'Field Calls' only, while his trumpet, which was used for 'Camp Calls', is slung across his back. Both instruments have 'Royal' cords and tassels, in mixed red, yellow, and blue worsted.

D1: Officer, 5th (Princess Charlotte of Wales's) Dragoon Guards; Undress.

*This officer is in a variant of No.5 'Drill Order', which, in accordance with Cavalry Division Orders of 8 August 1854, called for forage-caps and stable-jackets, arms, belts, and 'stripped saddles'. It would have been the normal everyday dress for wear around the camp. The blue cloth peaked cap, with its gold button on top and gold lace band, was a very popular item of wear in the Crimea. At home, the scarlet stable-jacket (which was also worn open over a waistcoat as an embryo form of mess kit) with its dark green velvet facings, and gold lace edging, was worn for dismounted duties around barracks in summer, while in winter the long dark blue frock coat was worn in its place. This latter seems never to have been worn in mounted orders of dress, when the men were in stable-jackets. The rest of the uniform, bridlery, and horse furniture is the same as has already been described. The Divisional Orders called for 'stripped saddles', which probably meant without cloaks and sheepskins (see **H1, 2, & 3**); but Vanson has several sketches of officers and men in undress uniform with these items, so it was probably a fairly common, if irregular, everyday turnout.*

D2: Sergeant, 6th (Inniskilling) Dragoons; Undress.

This Sergeant, like the figure of the officer above, is in a variant of No.5 'Drill Order'. Most of the sketches of cavalrymen in Undress by Vanson were made in Bulgaria, and it should be remembered that at the time of the battle most regiments did not have their stable-jackets with them. The forage-caps of the 6th Dragoons had a two-inch band of yellow cloth, and a yellow plaited worsted button on top which is not visible in this illustration. His stable-jacket has a yellow collar and pointed cuffs, the yellow shoulder straps being made from a piece of yellow worsted cord and fastened with a regimental button. His gold Sergeant's stripes, on their yellow cloth backing, can be seen on the right upper arm. He wears the usual blue booted overalls with a single yellow cloth stripe down the side, and he is armed with his sword, which is suspended from his waist-belt by two white buff leather slings. He is wearing his black sheepskin over his saddle, with his red cloak rolled in front.

D3: Corporal, 2nd or Royal North British Dragoons; Undress.

The Scots Greys, coming straight from Turkey, landed with all their baggage, which would have included their stable-jackets. This soldier, in the same order of dress as the two previous figures, wears the distinctive forage-cap of his regiment. Made of blue cloth, it has a red bobble or 'tourie' on top, and a white zig-zag (or 'Vandyked') line around the band. His stable-jacket has a blue collar and cuffs and yellow worsted shoulder straps. His two Corporal's chevrons, in yellow lace with a backing of blue cloth, can be seen on the right upper arm; and he wears the usual blue booted overalls with a single yellow cloth stripe. The white buff leather pouch-belt, with its brass buckle, slide, and tip, and its steel carbine swivel and clip, are clearly seen, as is the black leather pouch with its brass eagle badge. He holds his carbine with his right hand around the barrel and the butt resting on his right thigh, as he would when acting as a Vedette on outpost duty. Note the steel bar along the side of the carbine, and the steel ring which slid along it and was attached to the clip on the pouch-belt. His horse furniture is the same as that worn by the Inniskilling Dragoons Sergeant (D2).

A1: Troop Sergeant-Major, 5th (Princess Charlotte of Wales's) Dragoon Guards

A2: Officer, 4th (Royal Irish) Dragoon Guards

A3: Corporal, 5th (Princess Charlotte of Wales's) Dragoon Guards

B1: Private, 1st (Royal) Dragoons

B2: Officer, 1st (Royal) Dragoons

B3: Sergeant, 6th (Inniskilling) Dragoons

Plate C

C1: Officer, 2nd (Royal North British) Dragoons

C2: Private, 2nd (Royal North British) Dragoons

C3: Trumpeter, 2nd (Royal North British) Dragoons

D1: Officer, 5th (Princess Charlotte of Wales's) Dragoon Guards

D2: Sergeant, 6th (Inniskilling) Dragoons

D3: Corporal, 2nd (Royal North British) Dragoons

E1: Regimental Sergeant-Major,
4th (Queen's Own) Light Dragoons

E2: Officer, 4th (Queen's Own) Light Dragoons

E3: Sergeant, 13th Light Dragoons

F1: Officer, 11th (Prince Albert's Own) Hussars

F2: Troop Sergeant-Major,
11th (Prince Albert's Own) Hussars

F3: Corporal, 8th (The King's Royal Irish) Hussars

Plate G

G1: Officer, 17th Lancers

G2: Trumpeter, 17th Lancers

G3: Corporal, 17th Lancers

Plate H

H1: Troop Sergeant-Major, 13th Light Dragoons

H2: Private, 8th (The King's Royal Irish) Hussars

H3: Officer, 17th Lancers

COLOUR PLATES E – H

E1: Regimental Sergeant-Major, 4th (Queen's Own) Light Dragoons; 'Left Guard'.

The Light Dragoons landed in the Crimea on 15 September 1854 in No.8 'Patrol Order', but with dress jackets, without epaulettes and shoulder-scales, and with sheepskins but no baggage. The RSM of the 4th Light Dragoons wears his dress shako in its waterproof cover, attached to his body by means of the gold cord cap-lines, which are held close to his neck by plaited slides, and which end in two plaited acorns. His dress jacket has a red collar and pointed cuffs edged with gold lace; and the edges of his rank badges – four inverted gold chevrons, surmounted by a gold 'English' crown, all on red cloth – can just be made out on his right lower arm just above the cuff. The turnbacks of the jacket are red, and there is a short piece of gold fringe at the back of the waist. He wears a crimson and gold girdle, white gloves, and blue overalls with two gold lace stripes but without leather 'strappings'. As he is armed with a pistol as well as a sword, he wears the shortened pouch-belt over his left shoulder, over the straps of his canteen and haversack which hang down on his left side. His bridle has a brass crescent, or 'amulet', hanging from the end of the throat-lash — an item peculiar to the light cavalry; and his blue cloak can be seen strapped to the front of his saddle. In the 'Left Guard' position the arm was raised and the sword carried to the left, with the point downwards, 'the edge and point rather to the rear, the wrist being above, and in advance of the peak of the cap'.

E2: Officer, 4th (Queen's Own) Light Dragoons; 'Right Point'.

This figure is wearing a 'Foul-weather Cap' specially made up to simulate the dress shako in a waterproof cover. It has gilt rings at each side at the top, through which the gold and crimson cap-lines pass, and a solid black leather oval boss at the front, simulating the cockade on the front of the dress shako underneath the 'cover'. The gilt chin-chain is attached, at each side, to gilt lion's-head bosses. His dress jacket has a scarlet collar and pointed cuffs edged with gold lace, and further ornamented with gold Russia braid. He wears a gold lace girdle with two woven crimson silk stripes, white gloves, and blue booted overalls with double gold lace stripes. The sword-knot, looped around his right wrist, is of gold and crimson mixed cord, with a gold and crimson plaited acorn. He is wearing his white buff leather undress pouch-belt with a black leather pouch, and his black undress sword-belt. The head collar of his bridle is lined with scalloped scarlet cloth, and the amulet has a black horse-hair throat plume hanging from it. The black sheepskin has a scarlet scalloped edge, and his blue cloak and pistol holster can be seen projecting below it. 'Right Point' was a downward jabbing movement on the off-side, starting off with the hand close to the right shoulder, the knuckles and edge of the sword facing upwards.

E3: Sergeant, 13th Light Dragoons; 'Right Prove Distance'.

Although the facings of the 13th Light Dragoons were officially described as 'buff', for all practical purposes they were, in fact, white. The Sergeant shown here has his shako in its waterproof cover, attached to his body by the yellow worsted cap-lines. The brass lion's-head bosses and chin-chain are clearly seen. His dress jacket, without its brass shoulder-scales, has a plain white collar, pointed cuffs, and turnbacks, the latter having a piece of yellow worsted fringe at the waist. The three gold lace chevrons of his rank, on their white cloth backing, can be seen on the right upper arm. His webbing girdle is yellow, with two red lines woven into it, and fastens on the left side by means of brass toggles and cord loops. He wears white gloves; and the grey overalls, with double white cloth stripes down the side, issued as an experimental measure in March 1854. He carries his canteen and haversack on the left side. His carbine, with its muzzle resting in the carbine bucket, and secured round the small of the butt by the carbine strap, is further secured by being clipped on to the pouch-belt by means of the steel swivel and clip. His saddlery and horse furniture is similar to that worn by the RSM above (E1). 'Right Prove Distance' was carried out prior to performing the Sword Exercise as a safety measure, as 'an awkward man may occasion a severe accident by not exactly covering his file'.

F1: Officer, 11th (Prince Albert's Own) Hussars; 'Right Guard'.

When the Hussars landed in the Crimea they left their pelisses and stable jackets on board the transports, and wore their dress jackets. The officer's brown fur Hussar cap, with its crimson cloth bag and gilt lion's-head bosses and chin-chain, but without its white-over-crimson feather plume, is attached to the wearer's body by means of the crimson and gold cord cap-lines. The blue dress jacket with its heavy decoration, carried out in special regimental pattern gold lace, chain gimp, and Russia braid, is that of a Lieutenant or Captain, Field Officers being distinguished 'by a larger figure on the sleeve' and by wider lace round the collar, cuffs, and body. This officer wears his full dress pouch- and sword-belts, made of gold regimental lace on a crimson backing. His black undress sabretache hangs from his sword-belt, and his crimson and gold barrel sash is just visible underneath his bridle hand. He wears crimson booted overalls with double gold lace stripes down the side. His horse's head collar is lined with scalloped crimson cloth, the amulet has a crimson horse-hair throat plume, and his black sheepskin is edged with scalloped crimson cloth. In the 'Right Guard' position the sword was carried to the right, with the edge inclining to the rear, the point being advanced, the arm slightly bent with the knuckles turned upwards.

F2: Troop Sergeant-Major, 11th (Prince Albert's Own) Hussars; 'Engage'.

The brown fur Hussar cap, with its crimson cloth bag and brass lion's-head bosses and chin-chain, but without its white-over-crimson horse-hair plume, is attached to the wearer by gold cord cap-lines ending in gold plaited acorns. His dress jacket has gold cord decoration, and on his right arm he wears the four gold lace chevrons, ordered to be worn by Troop Sergeant-Majors of Hussars only in the Circular Memorandum for Cavalry *dated 22 May 1850, surmounted by the 'Regimental Badge' laid down for the 11th: a gold embroidered Guelphic Crown, all on a crimson cloth backing. These extra badges, which were to be worn by Sergeants as well, were not to be worn by them on the undress jacket. He wears a crimson and gold barrel sash; and his short white buff leather pouch-belt over the left shoulder, passing over his canteen and haversack straps which pass to his left side. His waist-belt is fitted with a white buff leather percussion cap-pouch on the right side of the brass belt-plate. His crimson overalls, with their double gold lace stripes, are without strappings. His horse's bridle has a brass amulet hanging from the throat-lash; and his 'high mounting' Hussar sadle, with its spoon cantle projecting through the black sheepskin, is clearly seen, with his blue cloak rolled in front and his grey camp blanket behind. The 'Engage' was the first movement of the Sword Exercise proper; the hilt of the sword was to be brought to the pit of the stomach, the edge to the left, and the point advanced.*

F3: Corporal, 8th The King's Royal Irish (Light) Dragoons (Hussars); 'Cut Three'.

This figure has the usual brown fur Hussar cap, but with his regiment's red cloth bag, and without its white-over-red horse-hair plume. It is attached to the wearer by yellow worsted cap-lines. Some of Vanson's sketches, done in Bulgaria, show men of the Hussar regiments with their fur caps in white covers with neck flaps. At home Hussars wore their dress jackets from April to October, and their pelisses from October to April, and would — like the always correctly dressed Lord Cardigan — have worn their pelisses on the day of the battle, had they not been left on the transports. The Corporal's dress jacket has a blue collar and cuffs like the 11th, and is ornamented with yellow worsted cord; this is also used, instead of lace, to make up the two chevrons, on their red cloth backing, on his right upper arm. The yellow worsted toggle which fastened the crimson and yellow barrel sash can be seen at the wearer's waist at the back. He is without gloves; and wears blue overalls with a single yellow stripe down the side, but without strappings. He carries his canteen and haversack on the left side, with their straps passing under his white buff leather pouch-belt, with its plain black leather pouch. His black leather sabretache can be seen suspended from his waist-belt by its two white buff leather slings. 'Cut Three' was a forehand cut, starting off with the sword perpendicular and the edge to the rear, the wrist being as high as the shoulder, and then cutting low, with a sweeping motion, from rear to front, on the off-side of the horse.

G1: Officer, 17th Light Dragoons (Lancers); 'Fourth Guard'.

This officer wears a specially made 'Foul-weather Cap', simulating the traditional square-topped Lancer cap or chapska *in its waterproof cover. On the top left front can be seen the solid black leather boss representing the large cockade underneath the 'cover'. The cap has a false buttoned opening down the left side, gilt lion's-head bosses and chin-chain, and is attached to the wearer by the gold cord cap-lines. These pass around the body four times, over the right shoulder and under the left arm, the two gold acorn ends finishing up hooked to the top left button of the jacket. The dress jacket has a plain white collar, pointed cuffs, and turnbacks, together with white piping on the back seams of the sleeves and body. His gold and crimson lace girdle would probably have (as in Cornet Wombwell's case) the gold embroidered and fringed decoration, which normally went on the jacket, sewn to the back part. He wears white buff leather gauntlets, grey booted overalls with double white cloth stripes, the dress gold lace pouch–belt with its silver chains and pickers, and his dress waist-belt. His horse's collar headstall is lined with red scalloped cloth and has an amulet with a red horse-hair throat plume. His black sheepskin is also lined and edged with red scalloped cloth. For the 'Fourth Guard' the knuckles were turned outwards, the edge to the rear and the point to the front, so as to defend the leg.*

G2: Trumpeter, 17th Light Dragoons (Lancers).

This figure wears his dress cap in its waterproof cover, with its lion's-head bosses and chin-chain fastened on the outside, and is attached to his body by the yellow worsted cap-lines. His dress jacket, shorn of its brass shoulder-scales, has a plain white collar, pointed cuffs, and turnbacks with a small piece of yellow worsted fringe at the back. The back seams of the jacket are piped in white. He wears the usual yellow and red webbing girdle, white buff leather gauntlets, and the experimental grey overalls issued to the regiment in March 1854, with double white cloth stripes. He wears his pouch-belt over his left shoulder, and his canteen and haversack on his left hip. His saddlery and horse furniture are of the normal light cavalry pattern, with the brass amulet hanging from the throat lash. He is sounding a call on his bugle which, like the trumpet slung on his back, has mixed red, yellow, and blue worsted cords and tassels. The whole matter of whether any of the Trumpeters, of either Brigade, sounded their bugles during the battle has been hotly debated. The majority of those survivors who joined in the discussion agreed that no soundings of any description took place; while others maintain that the 'Walk!', 'Trot!' and 'Gallop!' only were in fact sounded by Trumpeter William Britten, 17th Lancers, who was Lord Cardigan's Orderly Trumpeter during that week, and who was mortally wounded during the charge.

G3: Corporal, 17th Light Dragoons (Lancers); 'Left Point and Parry'.

This figure is in modified No.8 'Patrol Order', as he would have appeared on the day of the battle. His lance cap in its waterproof cover is attached to his body by the yellow worsted cap-lines. In Turkey and Bulgaria the cap was worn with a white cover and neck-flap. His dress jacket is without its brass shoulder-scales. The collar, pointed cuffs, turnbacks, and piping to the back seams are all white. His two yellow worsted lace chevrons, on their white cloth backing, on his right upper arm, and the yellow worsted fringe on the waist at the back, can be clearly seen. He wears the usual yellow and red webbing girdle, white buff leather gauntlets, and grey overalls with double white cloth stripes. His short white buff leather pouch-belt and black leather pouch are worn over the left shoulder, and the straps of his water canteen and haversack over his right shoulder. His saddlery and horse furniture are as shown in G2 above, with the addition of the brown leather lance buckets, which were attached by narrow leather straps and buckles to loops welded on to the sides of both stirrup irons, and into which the butt of the lance was normally placed. Note the red and white lance pennon, and the white buff leather arm-strap at the point of balance. The 'Left Point and Parry' involved holding the lance at the point of balance with the right hand, and bringing it across the horse's neck to the near-side.

H1: Troop Sergeant-Major, 13th Light Dragoons; Undress.

This figure is in No.5 'Drill Order'. His blue forage-cap has a gold plaited button on top, and a wide gold lace band. His undress jacket has a white collar and pointed cuffs edged with gold lace, and gold cord shoulder-straps. On his right upper arm he wears the badge of three gold lace chevrons, on a white cloth backing, surmounted by an embroidered Crown, as laid down for Troop Sergeant-Majors in regiments other than Hussars. He wears white gloves, and grey overalls with a double gold stripe. He is armed with a single pistol, the butt of which can be seen projecting out of his off-side holster, and the ammunition for which is carried in the pouch on his white buff leather pouch-belt, together with a sword, which hangs on the near-side. He has the normal light cavalry saddlery and horse furniture, but as 'stripped saddles' were called for in 'Drill Order' his horse is shown without the rolled blue cloak in front of the saddle, the grey camp blanket behind the saddle, or the black sheepskin which normally covered up these items.

H2: Private, 8th The King's Royal Irish (Light) Dragoons (Hussars); Undress.

This figure is also in 'Drill Order'. His blue forage-cap has a yellow worsted button on top, not visible in this drawing, and a yellow cloth band. His undress jacket has a blue collar and pointed cuffs edged with yellow worsted cord. His shoulder-straps are made up from the same cord, as are his two good conduct chevrons, on their red cloth backing, sewn just above the cuff on his left arm. He wears blue overalls with a single yellow cloth stripe, and is armed with sword and carbine. As only Troop Sergeant-Majors, Trumpeters, and Other Ranks of Lancer regiments were armed with a single pistol, his saddle is fitted with a pair of brown leather wallets in place of pistol holsters. Cavalry Division Orders of 10 August 1854 laid down that in 'Patrol Order' one pair of shoes and two brushes were to be carried in these wallets. Otherwise his saddle is stripped, and the foraging cord, using to bundle up the provisions acquired when so engaged, can be seen attached to the spoon cantle.

H3: Officer, 17th Light Dragoons (Lancers); Undress.

The blue peaked forage-caps of the officers of the 17th Lancers had a gold plaited button on top, a gold lace band, and a gold-embroidered peak. In addition, the crown of the cap was quartered by lines of narrow gold Russia braid, crossing from front to back and from side to side. The undress jacket had a white collar and pointed cuffs which, together with the front edges and bottom of the jacket, were edged with gold lace. A narrow gold cord ran round the bottom of the collar, and similar cord formed the shoulder-straps. The white piping on the back seams, and the two 'nose-shaped' projections of padded gold lace (a traditional feature of Hungarian Hussar dress) where the back seams meet the bottom edge of the jacket, can be clearly seen. The officer shown here wears his gold lace dress pouch-belt, with its central white silk line or 'train' and silver fittings; his dress pouch, with its solid silver flap ornamented with a gilt VR and crown; white gloves; and grey booted overalls with a double white cloth stripe. His saddlery and horse furniture are the same as that shown in G1; but in this case, as he is in 'Drill Order', the saddle has been stripped to reveal the pistol holster, out of which protrudes the butt of his privately purchased revolver; and the general construction of his non-regulation, custom-built, Hussar saddle, which combines the fixed leather seat of the English hunting saddle with the high front and rear arches and the brass-edged spoon cantle of the Hungarian Hussar saddle.

Sergeant, trumpeter and privates, 13th Light Dragoons, in
marching order, c1854. Watercolour by Michael Angelo
Hayes. (Parker Gallery)

Sergeant, trumpeter and privates, 4th Light Dragoons, in
marching order, c1850. Oil painting, artist unknown.
(Queen's Royal Irish Hussars)

Lt.Col.Doherty with officers and men of the 13th Light Dragoons, spring 1855. Photograph by Roger Fenton. (National Army Museum)

Hussars

Although Light Dragoons had been partly clothed in Hussar fashion since 1784, true Hussars did not appear in the British Army until 1805, when the 7th, 10th, 15th, and 18th Light Dragoons were ordered to be clothed and equipped as Hussars. In the reduction of the cavalry after the Napoleonic Wars the 18th Hussars were disbanded, but in their place the 8th Light Dragoons were converted to Hussars in 1823. In 1840 the 11th Light Dragoons were called upon to furnish an escort for Prince Albert on his arrival in England for his wedding to Queen Victoria, and shortly after the Queen ordered that the regiment should be clothed and equipped as Hussars, and styled 'Prince Albert's Own'. Thus the two Hussar regiments in the Light Brigade were the most recent to have been converted to that rôle.

The uniform of Hussar regiments had changed very little since they were first introduced in 1805. With the exception of the 11th, who wore their famous cherry coloured overalls, and the 15th, who wore scarlet shakos, there was very little to distinguish one Hussar regiment from another. All wore red busby bags, red and white plumes, and blue collars and cuffs. Officers of the various regiments could be identified by their sabretaches, pouches and belts, and shabraques, each of which was of regimental pattern. When mounted, Other Ranks could be distinguished by their valises, marked with the regimental number, and their shabraque; but there was little to identify a Private when dismounted.

Officers' Dress Regulations reproduced from 'Dress Regulations for the Army 1846':

HUSSARS

DRESS.

Jacket—entirely of blue cloth; Prussian collar full three inches deep, laced round and ornamented with Russia braid; single-breasted, with five rows of buttons, centre row, balls, the others half balls; richly trimmed with dead gold gimp chain-loops, extending the full width of jacket across breast, and about three inches wide at bottom; the effect of the dead gold relieved by a looping of bright Russia braid, which intersects the other loops; pointed sleeve, about three inches deep at the point, laced round with regimental lace and ornamented with gold Russia braiding; edges of the jacket entirely laced round with regimental lace, which passes over the knobs behind, round the welts and side seams, which are also richly ornamented with Russia braid.

Pelisse—blue cloth, braided similarly to jacket, with gimp and Russia braid; collar and cuffs of fur according to regimental pattern, and a narrow edging of the same fur entirely round the pelisse, with inlets to the sleeves and welts; the sleeve, side-seams, welts, and hips, ornamented with gold lace and braiding; crimson silk lining, rich dead gold plaited necklines, relieved with bright gold sliders and olivet ends.

Field Officers distinguished by a larger figure on the sleeve, both of the jacket and pelisse.

Waistcoat—scarlet, with half-ball buttons, and ornamented with gold cord. (Not worn in the 8th or 11th Hussars.)

Cap—busby, or regimental fur, nine inches deep, and the same size at top and bottom; scarlet* fly and plaited top (sunk an inch and a half within the edge of the fur); gilt chain fastening to lions' heads at the sides; gold line with olives†.

Plume—white egrette with scarlet* bottom, ten inches high; gilt socket and ring.

Trousers—blue cloth, with a stripe of gold lace, one inch and a half wide, down the outward seam††.

* Crimson, in the 11th Hussars.

† The 15th Hussars have permission to wear a scarlet cloth chaco, according to regimental pattern. The 10th Hussars, while serving in India, will wear a chaco, of regimental pattern.

†† The 10th and 11th Hussars are permitted to wear *two stripes* of gold lace, each three quarters of an inch wide, with a light between; and the trousers of the 11th Hussars are crimson.

(continued on page 82)

The Hussars, 1846: 8th, 10th and 11th Regiments of Light Dragoons (Hussars) with vignettes of other regiments around the border. Lithograph after Michael Angelo Hayes, no.5 in the series The British Army. (Parker Gallery)

Major General The Earl of Cardigan in review order, 11th Hussars, 1855. Oil painting by A.F.de Prades. (National Army Museum)

Officer, trumpeter and privates in review order, 8th Hussars, c1850. Oil painting by Henry Martens. (Parker Gallery)

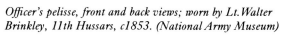

*Officer's jacket, front and back views,
8th Hussars, 1829- 55.
(National Army Museum)*

*Officer's pelisse, front and back views; worn by Lt. Walter
Brinkley, 11th Hussars, c1853. (National Army Museum)*

Officer's busby, 8th Hussars, c1850. (National Army Museum)

Boots—ankle.

Spurs—gilt, with two-inch necks and rowels.

Sword—steel mounted, half-basket hilt, with two fluted bars on the outside; black fish-skin gripe, bound with silver wire; the blade very little curved, thirty-five inches and a half long and one inch and a quarter wide, with a round back, terminating within eleven inches of the point.

Scabbard—steel, with large shoe at the bottom, solid bands, and rings; a trumpet-formed mouth.

Sword-Knot—gold and crimson, with a large acorn.

Sash—gold and crimson barrelled; large acorns at the ends of the cord.

Belt—gold lace, one inch and a quarter wide, with scarlet morocco edging and lining, fastened in front with a clasp ornament; gilt mountings, and three rings, from which hang two sword-slings of similar width, with loops and buckles for rings of scabbard, and three half-inch tache-slings, with loops and buckles for rings of tache.

Lt.Col.John Douglas, 11th Hussars, in review order, c1856. Photograph. (Royal Hussars)

Sabre-Tache—scarlet cloth* face, laced with gold lace, two inches and a quarter wide, leaving an edge of scarlet; embroidered regimental badge in the centre; three gilt rings at top; pocket, scarlet morocco.

Pouch-Belt—gold lace, one inch and a half wide, scarlet cloth edging, and morocco lining; gilt ornamented buckle, tip and slide; attached to sides of pouch†.

Pouch-Box—scarlet cloth; circular flap, five inches deep, six inches wide at top, six and half at bottom,edged round with gold braid and embroidery; embroidered regimental badge in centre*.

Stock—black silk.

Gloves—white leather.

* In the 11th Hussars, the cloth face and morocco pocket of the sabretache, and the lining and edging of the belts, are crimson instead scarlet; and a pouch-box is sanctioned, of gilt metal with silver ornaments, according to regimental pattern.

† The 10th Hussars are permitted to wear, both in dress and undress, a pouch and pouch belt, of black patent leather, according to regimental patterns.

UNDRESS

Trousers—blue cloth, with a yellow stripe, one inch and a half wide, down the outward seam.

Sword-Knot—of regimental pattern.

Sabre-Tache
Belt†† } black patent leather, with
Pouch } gilt mountings.
Pouch-Belt

†† In the 10th and 11th Regiments, Russia leather.

Jacket
Pelisse
Waistcoat
Cap
Boots
Spurs } As in DRESS.
Sword
Scabbard
Sash
Stock
Gloves

Stable-Jacket—blue; single-breasted, with olivets and gold lace according to regimental pattern.

Frock-Coat—blue cloth, with loops, olivets, and braiding, according to regimental pattern; in the 7th, 10th, and 15th Regiments, a rolling collar;in the 8th and 11th Regiments, a stand-up collar; pointed cuff, with ornamental figure upon the sleeve.

Forage-Cap—blue cloth; a gold band, one inch and three quarters wide, a gold braided ornament and purl button at top; the seam of the crown of the cap encircled with gold braid; gold embroidered peak, and oil-skin cover*.

Cloak—blue cloth, lined with scarlet; except in the 8th Regiment, where the lining is white, and in the 11th where it is crimson.

* The forage cap in the 11th Hussars, is of crimson cloth, and in the 15th, of scarlet.

REGIMENTAL STAFF.

The Adjutant is to wear the uniform of his rank.

The Dress and Undress of the other officers of the Regimental Staff are to be the same as those worn by the rest of the officers, except that the sash is not to be worn, and that these officers wear, in the 8th and 11th Hussars, black cap-lines instead of gold, and in the 15th Hussars, the chaco without gold ornaments.

Officer's barrel sash, 8th Hussars, c1850. (National Army Museum)

Officer's overalls, 8th Hussars, c1850. (National Army Museum)

Additional items not fully described in the Dress Regulations:

Jackets—The Dress jackets of all ranks of the 11th Hussars had sloped back front edges to the collars, as had been the case with all collars in the British Army until the 1822 *Dress Regulations* introduced the closed 'Prussian' collar.

Sabretaches and Pouches—

8TH HUSSARS

Sabretache—Scarlet cloth face; gold lace; gold embroidered crown, lion, harp, and scrolls. Silver embroidered cypher, shamrock, and wording on scrolls.

Pouch—Colouring as sabretache, four-and-a-half inches high by six-and-a-half inches wide at the widest point.

Pouch-belt—Gold shamrock pattern lace on scarlet cloth backing. Gilt buckle, tip, and slide.

11TH HUSSARS

Sabretache—Crimson cloth face; gold lace and embroidery; blue velvet scrolls with gold lettering; silver metal sphinx.

Pouch—Gilt metal with applied silver decoration. Three-and-a-half inches high by six-and-three-quarter inches wide.

Pouch-belt—Gold regimental pattern lace on crimson leather backing; silver buckle, slide and tip; silver pickers and chains.

Rank and File

Jacket—Entirely of blue cloth; Prussian collar, two-and-three-quarter inches high, except in the 11th where the collar was open with sloping front edges, edged round and ornamented with yellow worsted cord; single-breasted, with three rows of buttons, 18 to a row; the centre row full ball buttons, the other two half-balls; trimmed with yellow worsted cord, extending the full width of the jacket across the breast, and about three inches wide at the bottom; pointed cuffs, edged round with yellow worsted braid, forming a trefoil at the point, with an inner line of a narrower yellow braid terminating in three eyes; the jacket edged all round with yellow cord, which passed over the knobs behind, round the welts, and side seams, where it was formed into eyes terminating in trefoil loops; false side pockets edged with yellow worsted cord ending in trefoil knots. Sergeant-Majors had gold lace and cord in place of yellow worsted.

Pelisse—Blue cloth; ornamented in a similar manner to the jacket with yellow worsted cord; collar and cuffs of false black fur, with a narrow band of the same edging the pelisse, with inlets to the cuffs and welts; red serge lining; yellow worsted cord lines with woven toggle, slides, and acorns.

Badges of Rank—Gold lace for Sergeant-Majors and Sergeants (Sergeant-Majors of Hussars having four chevrons) and yellow worsted cord for Corporals, each chevron on a backing of the facing colour. Sergeant-Majors' and Sergeants' chevrons were surmounted by a gold embroidered Guelphic, or 'Hussar' Crown, the 8th Hussars having, in addition, a silver embroidered Harp between the Crown and the chevrons. The Crowns and Harp were not worn by Sergeants on their undress jackets.

Officer's full dress sabretache and pouch, 8th Hussars, 1848-55. (Mollo Collection)

Officer's full dress sabretache and pouch, 11th Hussars. 1840-55. (McAlpine Collection)

Good Conduct Badges—Yellow worsted cord, each chevron on a backing of the facing colour.

Trumpeters—Trumpeters of the 8th Hussars seem to have had their uniforms trimmed with red and yellow mixed cord; and the 11th with crimson and yellow mixed cord. In addition the Trumpeters of the 11th had grey busbies, but it is not clear whether or not these distinctive items were left behind, on embarkation for the East.

Farriers—Badges, consisting of a horseshoe embroidered in yellow worsted (gold for Farrier-Majors), on a backing of the facing colour, were worn on the right upper arm of the jacket.

Sash—Crimson worsted cord, with yellow woven barrels, slides, and acorns.

11th Hussars, church parade order, 25 March 1855; back view of officer wearing pelisse. Pencil drawing by General Vanson. (Musée de l'Armée)

11th Hussars, review of effectives, March 1855; officer wearing forage cap and pelisse. Pencil drawing by General Vanson. (Musée de l'Armée)

Troop sergeant-major's jacket worn at Balaclava by TSM Loy Smith, 11th Hussars. The label is attached to a button of the Russian 11th Kievski Hussar Regiment picked up on the field of Balaclava. (City Museum Sheffield)

Cap—Busby, similar in dimensions to those of the Officers, but made of cheaper and less substantial fur; scarlet cloth bag for the 8th Hussars, crimson for the 11th; brass lions'-heads and chin-chains; yellow worsted cord lines, with yellow woven slides and acorns.

Plume—White over red for the 8th Hussars, white over crimson for the 11th, made of hair, approximately six inches in height.

Trousers—Dark blue cloth, with a single yellow cloth stripe down the outside seams, for the 8th Hussars; crimson cloth with double yellow cloth stripes for the 11th; the stripes being three-quarters of an inch wide with a narrow light in between. Sergeant-Majors had gold lace stripes.

Boots—Ankle.

Spurs—Steel.

Stock—Black leather.

Trumpeter with officer's charger, troop formed up in background; 11th Hussars, 1847. Oil painting by E.Brown, signed and dated. (Parker Gallery)

Troop Sergeant Major Kilvert, 11th Hussars, in review order, c1855. Oil painting, artist unknown. (Royal Hussars)

Undress

Forage-cap—Red cloth for the 8th, crimson for the 11th, with a two-inch wide yellow cloth band; yellow woven button on top; black leather chin-strap with adjusting buckle.

Stable-jacket—Blue; single-breasted with nine regimental full ball buttons in front; blue collar and pointed cuffs, edged with yellow worsted cord; open slit at the base of the sleeve closing with two regimental buttons; yellow cord shoulder straps with buttons. Sergeant-Majors had gold cord in place of yellow worsted.

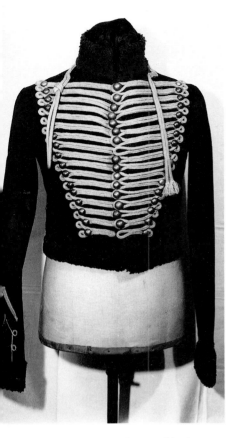

*Private's pelisse, front and back views,
15th Hussars, marked in lining '1852'.
(L. & H. Nathan Ltd.)*

*Private in review order, 8th Hussars, c1850. Oil painting,
artist unknown. (Mollo Collection)*

*Private's barrel sash, Hussar Regiments,
c1850. (L. & H. Nathan Ltd)*

Sergeant Bruse,
11th Hussars, c1856.
Photograph. (Parker Gallery)

Lancers

Lancers first made their appearance in the British Army in 1816 and 1817, when the 9th, 12th, 16th, and 19th Light Dragoons were converted to that arm. The 19th were disbanded in 1821, and the following year their place was taken by the 17th Light Dragoons, who were to be the only Lancer regiment in the Light Brigade.

The uniform worn by the 17th in 1854 dated back to the changes of 1829-30. With other light Cavalry regiments the 17th had been ordered to adopt red jackets in 1830, but had reverted to blue in 1838. The Lance Cap had been reduced considerably in size and richness over this period, but in other respects there was little change in their overall appearance.

The different Lancer regiments could be distinguished in the following ways:—

1. The design of the dress Lance Cap varied from one regiment to another, each having the cloth of the square crown in a distinctive colour, as well as individual regimental pattern cap plates.

2. The facing colour on collar, cuffs, and skirt turnbacks of the jacket. The 16th Lancers retained the red jacket after 1830.
   9th and 12th Lancers — scarlet.
   16th Lancers — dark blue.
   17th Lancers — white.

3. Sabretaches and shabraques, which were embroidered with regimental distinctions

4. Buttons of regimental design.

Officers' Dress Regulations reproduced from 'Dress Regulations for the Army 1846':

LANCERS.
DRESS.

Jacket—blue; double-breasted, two rows of buttons, nine in each row, placed at equal distances; Prussian collar, three inches deep; two gold embroidered button holes, five inches long, at each end; pointed cuff, with an edging of embroidery, three quarters of an inch deep round the top; plaited skirt, seven inches in length, three inches and a half wide at bottom; gold bullion back-pieces; the collar, cuffs, turnbacks, and welts in the sleeve and back-seams, of the regimental facing*.

Epaulettes—cloth strap, of the colour of the regimental facing, richly embroidered with gold, bright bullion two inches and a half deep.

Cap—cloth; colour of the facings, eight inches and three quarters deep in front, nine inches and a half at back, and the top nine inches and a half square; gold cord across the top and down the angles; on left side a gold bullion rosette, with embroidered V.R., on blue velvet; round the waist a band, two inches wide, of gold lace, with a blue stripe; in front a gilt ray plate, with silver Queen's arms and regimental badges; peak and fall of black patent leather, braided with gold; gilt chain, fastening to lions' heads at the sides†.

* The 16th Lancers wear a scarlet jacket, with welts of the same, a blue cuff and scarlet slashed flap on the sleeves, with five small buttons; and, instead of bullion back-pieces, two buttons at the hip, and slashed flaps on the skirt, each with three buttons.

† The 9th Lancers have permission to wear a cap of the regimental pattern, with gilt metal ornaments.

Cap Line—gold cord, with bullion tassels and flounders, to pass round the body, and to be secured to the back of the cap by a loop.

Plume—black drooping cocktail feathers, fourteen inches long, and four inches on the mount: in India, black horse-hair of the same length.

Trousers—blue cloth, with two stripes down each outward seam, of gold lace, three quarters of an inch wide, leaving a light between.

Boots—ankle.

Spurs—yellow metal, two inches long, with dumb rowels.

Sabre—steel mounted, half-basket hilt, with two fluted bars on the outside, black fish-skin gripe bound with silver wire; the blade very little curved, thirty-five

The Lancers, 1846: 12th, 16th and 17th Regiments of Light Dragoons (Lancers) with vignettes of other regiments around the border. Lithograph after Michael Angelo Hayes, no.6 in the series The British Army. *(National Army Museum)*

inches and a half long, and one and a quarter wide, with a round back, terminating within eleven inches of the point.

Scabbard—steel, with large shoe at the bottom, solid bands and rings; a trumpet-formed mouth.

Sword-Knot—gold and crimson cord strap, with acorn.

Girdle—gold lace, two and a half inches wide, with two crimson silk stripes.

Waist-Belt—gold lace, one and a quarter inch wide, with quarter-inch silk stripe up centre; morocco lining and edging, fastening in front with a snake-ornament; two large and one smaller gilt rings, from which hang three slings of one inch silk and gold vellum lace, by which tache is suspended, and two one-and-quarter inch gold and silk lace slings for sabre, all fastening with gilt buckles and leather straps; the silk stripes, and morocco lining and edging, to be of the colour of the regimental facing.

Sabre-Tache—purple leather pocket, thirteen inches and a half deep, ten and a half wide at bottom, eight at top; cloth face, colour of regimental facing, fourteen and a half deep, twelve wide at bottom, eight and a half at top, edged round with two and a quarter inch gold lace, showing a cloth edge; embroidered scroll, with regimental badge on velvet at bottom; above this, gold embroidered V.R., surmounted by a crown*.

Pouch-Belt—gold lace, two inches wide, with half-inch silk stripe, morocco lining and edging, to correspond with waist-belt; silver plate with pickers and chains, buckle, tip, and slide.

Pouch-Box—scarlet leather; a gold embroidered edging round the top; solid silver flap, seven inches and a half wide, two and three quarters deep, ornamented with gilt raised solid V.R. and crown; attached to belt by staples and rings†.

Stock—black silk.

Gloves—white leather gauntlets.

* The sabretache of the 9th Lancers has a double cypher A.R. The 17th Lancers wear no sabretache.

† The pouch box of the 9th and 17th Lancers is blue leather instead of scarlet, and that of the 9th has the double cypher A.R.

UNDRESS

Cap—oiled silk, shape and dimensions as *Dress* Cap; gilt chain, lined with black velvet.

Trousers—blue cloth, with two scarlet †† stripes, three quarters of an inch wide, down each outward seam, showing a light between.

†† In the 17th Lancers the stripes are white, the colour of the regimental facings.

Spurs—steel; two inches and a quarter long, including sharp rowels.

Waist-Belt—in the 9th Lancers, brown morocco leather,

Lt.Sir William Gordon Bt., 17th Lancers, c1856. Oil painting, artist unknown. (17th/21st Lancers)

with regimental ornaments: in the 16th, black patent leather; in the 12th and 17th, *as in dress.*

Sabre-Tache—black patent leather, pocket nine inches and a half deep, eight inches and a half wide at top, seven and a half at bottom; face, eleven inches and a half deep, ten and a half wide at bottom, seven at top; gilt chased ornament in the centre.

Jacket
Epaulettes
Boots
Sabre
Scabbard } As in DRESS.
Sword-Knot
Pouch-Belt
Pouch-Box
Stock

Gloves—white leather

Unidentified officer, 17th Lancers, in review order, c1854.
Watercolour, artist unknown. (Mollo Collection)

Stable-Jacket—blue round jacket, single-breasted, with small gilt studs quite close down the front, fastening with hooks and eyes; Prussian collar, three inches deep, pointed cuff, and welts in the sleeves and back seams, all of the regimental facing; a trimming of gold lace entirely round the jacket, and round the top of the cuff; the lace of the Field Officers to be one inch and a half wide, that of the other officers, one inch*.

* The stable jacket of the 16th Lancers is scarlet, with welts of the same, and the cuff is like that of their dress jacket.

Shoulder-Straps—gold cord.

Forage-Cap—blue cloth; a gold oak-leaf band, one inch and three quarters wide; a gold netted purl button at top, with gold braid crossing the top of the cap twice, and terminating under the lace band; gold embroidered peak, oil-skin cover.

Frock-Coat—blue, with braided loops.

Cloak—blue cloth, lined with scarlet; collar of regimental facing.

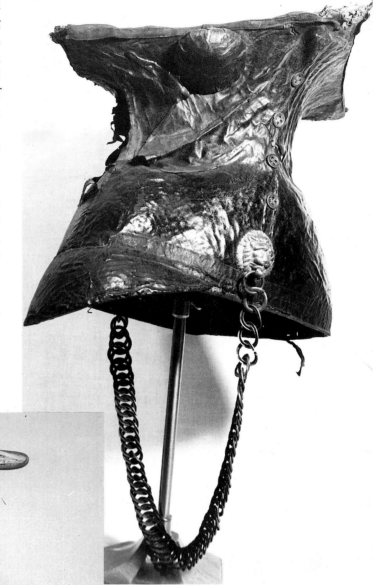

Officer's foul weather cap worn at Balaclava by Cornet George Wombwell, 17th Lancers. (Captain V.M. Wombwell)

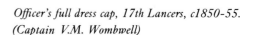

Officer's full dress cap, 17th Lancers, c1850-55. (Captain V.M. Wombwell)

Officer's jacket, front and back views, worn at Balaclava by Cornet George Wombwell, 17th Lancers. (Captain V.M. Wombwell)

REGIMENTAL STAFF

The Adjutant is to wear the uniform of his rank.

The Dress and Undress of the other officers of the Regimental Staff are to be the same as for other officers, except that the cap is to be without gold ornaments, and that the girdle is not to be worn.

Additional items not fully described in the Dress Regulations:

Officers' Lance Cap—White cloth crown; gold lace with a dark blue central 'train', around the narrowest part; gilt cap plate with silver applied ornament.

Pouch-Belt—Gold 'Broken Bias FS (Full scallop edged)' lace, with a white silk train; silver buckle, tip, slide, plates for chains and pickers, chains and pickers.

Buttons—Plain polished gilt, stamped with a skull over crossed bones.

Uniform changes between 1846 and 1854

By 1854 the Officers' cap had been reduced in size, being only eight inches high as opposed to the eight-and-three-quarter inches specified in the *Dress Regulations*. At the same time the top was reduced from nine-and-a-half inches square to eight-and-a-half inches square.

The *War Office Memorandum* of 27 November 1849, changing the colour of the Light Cavalry trouser stripes from red to yellow, did not affect the 17th, who already had white stripes, which they were permitted to retain.

In 1853 Officers of Lancer regiments were ordered to remove the gold embroidery from their collars and cuffs. By 1854, therefore, the 17th had plain white collars and cuffs even in full dress. A *Circular Memorandum* dated 18 April 1854 abolished sabretaches for all regiments except Hussars.

Rank and File

Jacket—Blue, of similar cut to that of the Officers but made of coarser material; plain white collar and pointed cuffs, skirt turnbacks, and piping on the back seams of the sleeves and body; two rows of eight pewter regimental buttons down the front; three on each skirt pocket flap; and two closing each sleeve above the cuff. A small piece of yellow worsted fringe

Sergeant, 17th Lancers; Hounslow,
12 March 1854. Watercolour by Wall.
(Anne S.K. Brown Collection)

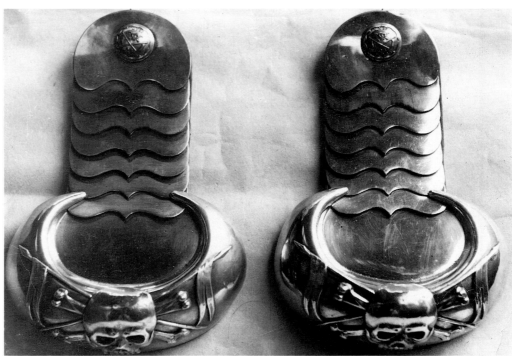

Other ranks' shoulder scales, 17th Lancers,
1829-55. (R.G. Harris Esq.)

Sergeant's full dress cap, 17th Lancers, c1850-55. (Army Museums Ogilby Trust)

*Private, 17th Lancers, in stable dress, with officer's charger,
c1854. Oil painting by E.Brown. (Christie's)*

(gold for Sergeant-Majors) was sewn to the waist of
the jacket at the back.

Shoulder-scales—Brass, with seven plain scales, and a
raised crescent, stamped with a skull and crossed
bones, attached by means of a regimental button and
a brass bridge sewn to the shoulders of the jacket.

Badges of Rank—Gold lace for Sergeant-Majors and Sergeants, and yellow worsted for Corporals, each chevron on a backing of the facing colour.

Good Conduct Badges—Yellow worsted lace on a backing
of the facing colour.

Trumpeter's Badge—Yellow worsted embroidered crossed
trumpets, on a backing of the facing colour, worn on
the right upper arm.

Farrier's Badge—Yellow worsted embroidered horseshoe
on a backing of the facing colour, worn on the right
upper arm.

Girdle—Yellow woven webbing, with two narrow red
stripes, fastening at the side with brass toggles and
cord loops.

Lance-cap—Black leather skull and peak; square upper
part of the body covered with white cloth; square
black leather top; broad yellow worsted lace with a
blue centre stripe, around the narrowest part of the
body; brass lion's-heads and chin-chain; stamped

brass plate with regimental devices. On the left front
of the top a blue and yellow woollen boss, with a
regimental button on the centre, holding a black
horsehair plume. Yellow worsted cord cap and body
lines, with woven slides and acorns.

Trousers—Blue cloth, with a double white stripe down the
outside seams, each stripe being three-quarters of an
inch wide, with a narrow light between. In March
1854 the 17th Lancers was one of four regiments
issued with experimental grey overalls, which they
wore when they embarked for the East.

Boots—Ankle.

Spurs—Steel.

Stock—Black leather.

Gloves—White buff leather gauntlets.

Undress

Forage-cap—Blue cloth with a two-inch white cloth band,
and a yellow woven button; black leather chin-strap
with adjusting buckle. Trumpeters had white forage
caps with a blue band and button.

Stable-jacket—Blue; single-breasted with nine pewter
regimental buttons in front; plain white collar and
pointed cuffs; yellow worsted cord shoulder-strap
(gold for Sergeant-Majors) with a regimental button,
on each shoulder. Trumpeters had stable jackets with
the back seams of the sleeves and body piped in white.

Equipment

The accoutrements of the Officers have already been described in their respective sections. Those of the Other Ranks, however, had no written description; and as very few, if any, actual examples have survived, information about them has to be gleaned from pictorial sources.

Pouch

Containing 20 rounds of ammunition for the pistol or carbine, this was made of black leather, with a loop at each side, and roller buckles underneath, to admit the two narrow straps from the pouch-belt. The flap was fastened by a small strap and a brass stud. While the pouches of the Light Cavalry were plain, those of the Heavy Cavalry, with the exception of the 6th Dragoons, had metal badges on the flap, as follows:—

4DG	Brass star of the Order of St. Patrick.
5DG	Brass eight pointed Star surmounted by a Crown.
1RD	Brass Crown.
2RNBD	Brass French Imperial Eagle.

Pouch-Belt

Worn over the left shoulder, of whitened buff leather, approximately two-and-three-eighths inches wide, with a rectangular brass buckle, slide, and tip. The belt formed one continuous loop, with a sliding steel swivel and clip for the carbine ring. Narrow buff leather straps, sewn to the inside of the belt, connected it to the pouch. The belts for Troop Sergeant-Majors of all regiments, Trumpeters, and all Other Ranks of the 17th Lancers, who were armed with pistols instead of carbines, were not continuous, but had rounded ends, to which were attached the two narrow pouch straps; they were without carbine clips and swivels.

Waist-Belt

Of whitened buff leather, approximately one and a half inches wide for the Light Cavalry, and slightly wider for the Heavy Cavalry, with a rectangular brass plate fastener, catch, and hook for hitching up the sword when dismounted. It was fitted with a long and a short sword carriage, approximately one inch wide, each with an oval brass adjusting buckle. For Hussars, there were in addition two sabretache slings, of similar width, each with an oval brass adjusting buckle. The Heavy Cavalry belt was fitted with a narrow strap and stud, on the left side, for securing the sword when it was hooked up. A variety of plates and clasps were worn, as follows:—

4DG	Brass rectangular plate with a Crown and Harp.
5DG	Brass rectangular plate with a Star.
1RD	Brass rectangular plate with a Crown.
2RNBD	Brass rectangular plate with a Thistle.
6D	Brass rectangular open buckle.
4LD	Brass rectangular plate with IV over LD.
8H	Brass snake clasp.
11H	Brass rectangular plate.
13LD	Brass rectangular plate.
17L	Brass rectangular plate.

Cap-Pouches

In addition to the percussion caps kept in the main pouch, a further twelve were kept for immediate use in a small leather pouch, or pocket, attached either to the waist-belt, or to the jacket, depending on the regiments:—

4DG	White buff leather pouch on the right front of the belt.
5DG	Black leather pocket on lower front of the jacket.
1RD	Black leather pocket on right lower front of dress and undress jackets.
2RNBD	White buff leather pouch below right front of belt.
6D	White buff leather on right front of belt.
4LD	White buff leather below right front of belt.
8H	White buff leather on right front of belt.
11H	White buff leather on right front of belt.
13LD	White buff leather on right front of belt.

Sabretache (Hussars only)

Of black leather, approximately eight-and-three-quarter inches wide at the top, nine-and-a-quarter inches wide at the bottom, and eleven-and-a-half inches high, with two brass D's on the top edge for the two sabretache straps.

Mess Tin

Roughly semi-circular in shape, six inches wide, four inches from front to back, and four inches deep. A three-and-seven-eights inch pan fitted inside, and there was a flanged cover. The mess tin was carried in the haversack in Marching Order.

Haversack

Made of a natural colour coarse linen, with a flap fastened with two buttons, it was worn over the right shoulder, over the pouch-belt, suspended from a strap of the same material. Vanson's drawings suggest that they were approximately fourteen inches deep by eight or nine inches wide.

Water Canteen

A circular wooden keg, bound with iron hoops, virtually unchanged since the Napoleonic Wars. Seven-and-a-quarter inches in diameter, and four inches deep, it held about half a gallon of water. It was unhygienic and heavy, comparing unfavourably with the French and Russian patterns. It was worn over the right shoulder, over the haversack, suspended from a one inch brown leather strap with a brass adjusting buckle. It was painted a mid to light blue, and was marked in white paint with the Broad Arrow and B.O. initials of the Board of Ordnance.

Blanket

The issue blanket was buff in colour, with a red line woven in it, and the Board of Ordnance mark, also in red.

Cooking Pot

Also known as a Camp Kettle; seven-and-a-half inches deep, ten inches in diameter at the top, and eight-and-a-half inches at the bottom, it was fitted with a bail handle, and a slightly countersunk lid.

Reconstruction of other ranks' equipment, Hussars, c1854. (Mollo Collection)

Saddlery and Horse Furniture

The various articles required to enable the horse to carry its rider, together with his equipment and weapons, came under the heading of Horse Appointments. Like his Accoutrements they were provided at the expense of the Colonel, and were supposed to last for a set period of time. There seems to have been a certain amount of latitude in the specification of the various items, and while the system worked well enough in peacetime, its general unsuitability in wartime caused it to be changed after the Crimean campaign when, with the exception of the Household Cavalry, Horse Appointments were provided by the Ordnance Department.

The *Standing Orders* of the 16th Lancers, 1852, list the various items then in use:—

Saddle-tree with Seat and Thongs and pair of Flaps.	14 years.
Saddle Blanket.	8 years.
Pilch.	8 years.
Girth and Strap.	9 years.
Crupper, with Buckles, Chapes, Dees, and Thongs.	9 years.
Leather Surcingle with Shabraque Straps.	9 years.
Breast Plate.	9 years.
Pair of Stirrup Leathers.	9 years.
Pair of Stirrup Irons.	20 years.
Pair of Holsters.	14 years.
Pair of Horse Shoe Cases with Straps.	9 years.
Pair of Lance Buckets.	12 years.
Middle Cloak Strap, and Pair of Double Cloak Straps.	9 years.
Set of three Baggage Straps.	12 years.
Pair of Farrier's Churns with Straps.	14 years.
Shabraque.	14 years.
Sheepskin.	10 years.
Bridle Bit with Curb Chains and Hooks.	20 years.
Bit Headstall with Nose-band and Bit Rein.	9 years.
Bridoon with Links and Tees.	9 years.
Bridoon Rein.	5 years.
Collar Headstall and Collar Chain.	5 years.

In addition, certain items of 'Cavalry Equipment' appear at the head of the list of Necessaries to be provided and maintained at the expense of the soldier:—

Valise.	Curry Comb.
Corn Bag.	Water Sponge.
Horse Log.	Horse Picker.
Horse Brush.	Pair of Scissors.
Web Surcingle.	

Regiments other than Lancers would have had a similar list, except that in their case the two pistol holsters were replaced by leather wallets, and they had a carbine bucket in place of the pair of lance buckets.

In preparing for Marching Order, the blanket went under the saddle, to which was attached the soldier's baggage in the following manner. The cloak, rolled neatly into a cylinder 40 inches long, was strapped to the holsters, or wallets, by means of the cloak straps, these last being in turn attached to the front arch of the saddle. The stable bag, containing one boot and one brush at each end, was fastened by the centre cloak strap, and was placed rather behind the holsters. The nearside holster contained the pistol, and the offside the curry comb, horse log, and sundry grooming equipment, with the forage cap tucked in between them. The corn bag, containing a clothes brush, was hung from the cantle on the offside, while the corn sack was placed over the saddle seat. The valise, which was attached to the rear of the saddle by means of the baggage straps, was packed with the soldier's spare clothing and towel. This had to be done extremely carefully, packing everything as far as possible at the ends of the valise, and keeping the centre empty so as to prevent it touching the horse's back. The shoe cases held, on the near side, a fore shoe and nails, horse picker and oil bottle; and on the off side, a hind shoe and nails, tin of blacking, piece of pipe clay and sponge. Over all this went the shabraque, the rear ends of which were turned up on the march to protect the embroidered badges from mud splashes; and over that the sheepskin, the whole being kept in place by the surcingle and shabraque straps. The muzzle of the carbine sat in its bucket on the front off side, and was held in place, when the soldier dismounted, by means of a small leather strap which came from the front arch of the saddle and passed round the small of the butt. The butt of the lance sat in a small leather bucket attached to both stirrups.

Saddles

The military rider, together with his weapons, accoutrements, baggage, and provisions, required a firm and comfortable saddle which would support his weight without transferring it to the horse's spine, where the skin was on the bone and rubbed through very easily. The care and maintenance of a regiment's saddlery was therefore of the greatest importance, and 'on the work of the Saddler, not less than that of the Farriers who kept the horses shod, depended to a very great extent the efficiency of the mounted men. A troop horse with a sore back, caused by an insufficiently stuffed saddle, was just as serious a loss to the fighting strength of an army as a man wounded by enemy action.'

Major J. Horton, writing in *The Cavalry Journal* in 1909, listed the essential features of a cavalry saddle. It had to be capable of carrying heavy equipments, in addition to the rider's weight; be of simple construction, and capable of adjustment; and it had to retain its serviceability under the roughest conditions of active service, knocking about, and exposure to bad weather, as well as the constant twists and strain inseparable from riding in the ranks in marching order.

Until 1805 there was a more or less standard pattern of saddle which was used by both Heavy and Light Dragoons, but in that year the Hungarian, or 'high-mounting', saddle was introduced for Hussars, and in 1812 it was adopted by the whole of the Light Cavalry. Thus, at the end of the Napoleonic Wars there were two types of saddle in use in the cavalry, and in spite of various modifications they were essentially the same in 1854.

The Heavy Cavalry saddle was the traditional English hunting saddle, with modifications for military service. It was lower in the seat than the Light Cavalry saddle, had curved front and rear arches, fans and burs (extensions to the sideboards, front and rear) to provide fixing points for various pieces of equipment, and points, or projections of the front arch below the sideboards, to prevent side-ways movement. The fixed seat was leather, and the cantle was bound in brass. A contemporary has described it as follows: 'The tree was as a hunting saddle, but much heavier with wood arches . . . it had long points but no burs and fans. The seat was of cowhide on stretched web or serge, padded with flock. Some seats were very short. The panels were heavily stuffed with flock, and in the Crimea a blanket was worn. Cruppers were used, and the girths, stirrups, and leathers, as well as the breast-plate were as issued with the Hussar or Light Cavalry saddle . . .'

The saddle used at Balaclava by Cornet Glyn of the Royals has fans and burs, a high peak, brass edging to the cantle, and knee-rolls; its weight, without panels, is ten pounds. In 1809 all saddles were ordered to be made of brown leather, and in 1834 Heavy Cavalry saddles were to have 'leather edged panels and pad, brass cantles, and a pair of bearing flaps'. In 1840 a new saddle was authorised for Heavy Cavalry, and a blanket was introduced to be worn under it. In 1845 there was an unspecified alteration, which was probably the introduction of the 'spoon cantle', which now projected through a hole in the sheepskin and shabraque. Nolan, in 1853, noted the improvements in the 'Hungarian saddle given to our Heavy Dragoons' namely, sideboards cut like those of a hunting saddle, a lower seat, a large blanket folded 12 times, and pads stuffed with horse-hair.

The Hungarian, or Hussar saddle, introduced into the British army in 1805, had high front and rear arches, from which was stretched a rawhide seat, laced to the sideboards with leather thonging. A separate quilted seat, or 'pilch', was attached by means of loops slipped over the spoon-shaped tops of the arches. The whole saddle came to pieces for cleaning and maintenance. Valentine Baker thought that the Hussar saddle would have been much lighter if it had not been so designed: 'Ordinary saddles never get out of order and are easily cleaned, and why a dragoon's should be such a complication of moveable straps and buckles, pilches, woofs etc. all made . . . like a Chinese puzzle, has ever been beyond my comprehension.'

The pattern in use in 1854, known as the Wood Arch, Pilch seat saddle, had changed little since 1805. The pilch seat was loose; a folded blanket was used; the girth was webbing, and permanently fixed to the bar on the off side; and the single buckle to the stirrup leather was worn low down, near the iron, with the spare end in a roll, to prevent the leather being cut by a sword blow.

The saddle used during the charge of the Light Brigade by Captain Morgan, 17th Lancers, has a fixed seat instead of the loose pilch, high front peak, spoon cantle, fans and burs, with the open pistol holsters still attached; it weighs 19 lbs 9 ozs.

Crupper

Intended to prevent the saddle sliding forward, this consisted of a leather strap with a loop at one end which passed under the horse's tail. The looped part was of rounded section, and where it joined the divided end of the main strap there were two ornamental bosses, of gilded metal for Officers, and brass for Other Ranks. The other end of the crupper was fastened to the rear arch of the saddle by means of a buckle.

Leather pistol holsters worn at Balaclava by Capt. Hutton, 4th Light Dragoons. (Parker Gallery)

Breast-plate

Intended to prevent the saddle sliding backwards, this consisted of three leather straps sewn together to form a Y. The two upper arms passed on either side of the horse's neck, and were fastened to the front of the saddle. The third strap passed underneath the body between the front legs, and was held in position by being buckled round the girth. At the junction of the three straps, over the front of the horse's chest, there was a heart-shaped patch surmounted by a metal boss.

Surcingle and Shabraque straps

The leather surcingle passed round the horse's body, over the sheepskin and shabraque, holding everything in position. The shabraque strap, of narrow leather, passed through loops on the inside of the surcingle, on each side, and thence round the outside of the pommel and cantle, holding the sheepskin and shabraque in place.

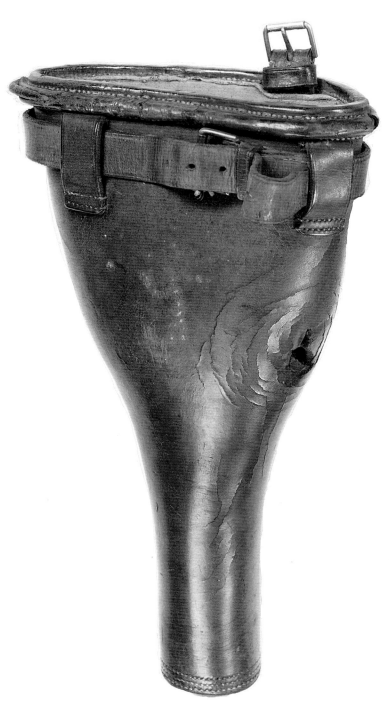

Stirrups

The leathers were attached to the sideboards, and passed over the top of the saddle flaps. The irons had curved bases, and narrowed in towards the top.

Holsters and Wallets

The holsters, open-topped, and made of stout leather, were attached to the front arch of the saddle by means of leather straps. In February 1840 pistols and 'holster-pipes' were discontinued, except for Sergeant-Majors and Trumpeters, who were to keep one pistol, and all N.C.O.s and men of Lancer regiments. The men of other regiments were to receive a pair of wallets instead. From the illustrations in Nolan's book on the training of cavalry remounts, these wallets seem to have been joined together at the top by a band of leather, and laid over the pommel of the saddle.

Horseshoe Cases

Small leather horseshoe-shaped pouches were carried behind the rider, one on each side, attached to the sideboards. In 1853 a uniform type of shoe was approved, varying in weight, depending on size, from 12 to 15 ounces. A minimum of six nails were to be used on the front shoes, and seven on the hind shoes.

Shabraque

This largely decorative item, which was not used in the Crimea, weighed some seven pounds, and was intended to keep the horse warm over the loins, and prevent the various articles of equipment rubbing its sides. It was placed over the saddle, and had a slit to allow the spoon cantle of the saddle to poke through. Those of the Heavy Cavalry were square-ended, in the regimental facing colour, edged with broad lace of regimental pattern, and with regimental devices on the front and hind quarters. Those of Light Dragoons and Lancers were blue with rounded ends; and those of Hussars red, crimson in the case of the 11th, with pointed ends.

Valise

This was a cylindrical cloth baggage case, red for Heavy Cavalry and blue for Light Cavalry, which opened along its long side, and was attached to the rear of the saddle by means of the three baggage straps. The circular ends of the valise were edged with lace, and were ornamented with the regimental number and initials, in yellow or white (silver or gold for officers) thus:—

4DG	Yellow lace and Roman IV over the letters DG
5DG	Yellow lace and Roman V over the letters DG
1RD	Yellow lace and Arabic 1 over the letters RD
2RD	Yellow lace and Arabic 2 over the letter D
6D	Yellow lace and Roman VI only
4LD	Yellow lace and Roman IV over the letters LD
8H	Yellow lace and Roman VIII over the letter H
11H	Yellow lace and Roman XI over the letter H
13LD	White lace and Roman XIII over the letters LD
17L	*Officers*: Silver lace and a silver embroidered skull and crossed bones.
	Other Ranks: White lace and Arabic 17 over the letter L

Sheepskin

A piece of black sheepskin covering the seat of the saddle, the cloak and holsters or wallets in front, and the valise behind, held in place by the surcingle and shabraque straps. Those of the officers were edged with scalloped red cloth (crimson in the case of the 11th Hussars).

Bit Headstall

Made of brown leather, this consisted of the bridlehead, with adjusting buckles, browband, throatlash, noseband, and reins. The curb bit had long swan-neck cheeks, and a high port in the mouthpiece, those of the Officers having a gilt crowned Garter, bearing a regimental device, on each side. The headstall had additional cross-pieces over the face, those of the Heavy Cavalry being arranged in a Y shape, and those of the Light Cavalry in an X, which were reinforced at various strategic points with metal bosses. The Heavy Cavalry headstall had, in addition, metal scales over the top of the bridlehead, and that of the Light Cavalry a brass crescent-shaped amulet hanging from the throat lash.

Collar Headstall

Made of brown leather, this was mainly used for securing the horse in bivouac, by means of the collar chain, one end of which was attached to the underside of the collar, and the other fastened round the horse's neck on the off side. A bridoon, or snaffle bit, together with a second set of reins could be attached to the collar headstall by means of a metal T-piece, and on certain duties, like watering order parades, the horse could be ridden with this alone. The collars of the officers were lined with red (crimson for the 11th Hussars) scallop-edged cloth.

Throat-plumes

Long horsehair plumes, in regimental colours, were worn attached to the throatlash of the officers' bridle headstall in certain orders of dress. Vanson usually shows officers in the Crimea without them, although they do appear in one or two photographs of officers of the 11th Hussars, taken by Fenton in 1856.

Weapons

The Sword Exercise

The cavalry recruit was taught to handle his sword on foot, and then, when he had acquired a reasonable proficiency, mounted. He was taught the basic drill movements of the draw, carry, and slope, and then to control his weapon in attack and defence, according to the principles first set down in the *Rules and regulations for the Sword Exercise of the Cavalry, 1796*. These consisted of the six offensive cuts, later increased to seven, and the seven defensive guards, designed to protect both horse and rider. Finally there was the Point, or Thrust, given with the nails up or down, and the Parry, a circular motion of the blade.

The sword exercise was taught in a formal style, with great regard for regularity, each cut being followed, in correct sequence, by its corresponding guard. 'And how came you to get this ugly cut', a doctor asked a wounded trooper of the Heavy Brigade. 'I had just cut five at the Russian', he replied with much warmth, 'and the d-d fool never guarded at all, but hit me over the head'.

The Heavy Brigade, unable to pierce the heavy Russian greatcoats, with their hatchet-pointed swords, used the edge, and inflicted some appalling wounds on the heads of the Russians, in some cases cleaving the shako and skull down to the chin. The British, in their turn, received an incredible number of cuts, a private of the 4th Dragoon Guards having 15 to his head, none of which was more than skin deep.

Heavy Cavalry Officers' Sword

The 1834 pattern sword, which was an early example of what is known as the 'Honeysuckle' hilt, with a 35-inch blade and steel scabbard, was still in use. The steel hilt had a back-piece with two ears which overlapped the leather-covered wooden grip, and a white buff leather lining. The blade had a hatchet point which made it extremely difficult to use as a thrusting weapon. The sword knot was of crimson and gold cord with a crimson and gold woven acorn-shaped knot.

Heavy Cavalry Other Ranks' Sword

The new pattern sword, approved in 1822, did not come into general use until about 1830. The hilt consisted of a steel bowl-shaped guard, with a leather-covered wooden grip, and a white buff leather liner. The blade, which was slightly curved, ended in a hatchet point; the steel scabbard had two rings to take the sword belt carriage straps; and the sword knot was of white buff leather.

Light Cavalry Officers' Sword

The 1822 pattern sword was still in use in 1854, and did not finally disappear until 1896. It had a steel three bar hilt, with a fishskin-covered wooden grip bound with silver wire. The scabbard was steel with two rings, and the sword knot was of crimson and gold cord ending in a woven acorn.

Light Cavalry Other Ranks' Sword

The 1829 pattern was still in use. This had a steel three bar hilt, with a leather-covered wooden grip, and a steel backpiece with two ears which overlapped the grip. The steel scabbard had two rings, and the sword knot was of white buff leather.

The Lance Exercise

As with the Sword Exercise, the whole of the Lance Exercise was taught on foot before the recruit attempted to perform it on horseback. He was first taught the basic drill movements, the shoulder and carry when dismounted, and the carry, trail, slung, and at ease positions when mounted. The Lance Exercise, first established in 1816, was divided into three 'Divisions'. The first consisted of guards against cavalry (22 motions), the second guards against infantry (18 motions), and the third (15 motions) contained the waves and points, the round parry, and the 'St George', or Head Protect, which was achieved by spinning the lance horizontally above the head with the arm extended. When using the pistol the

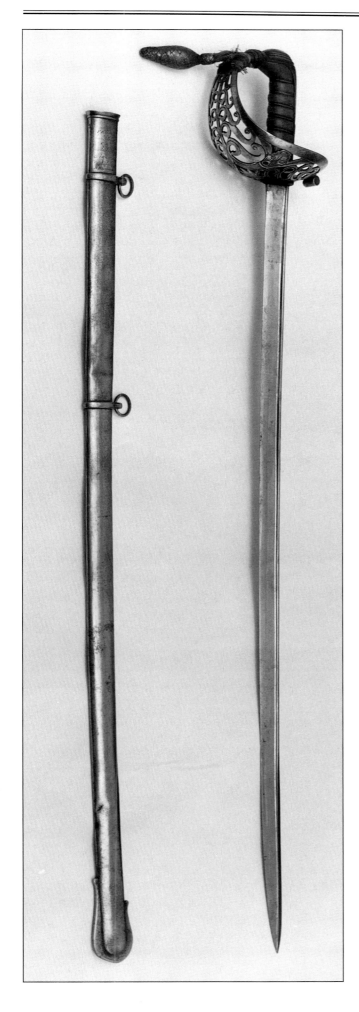

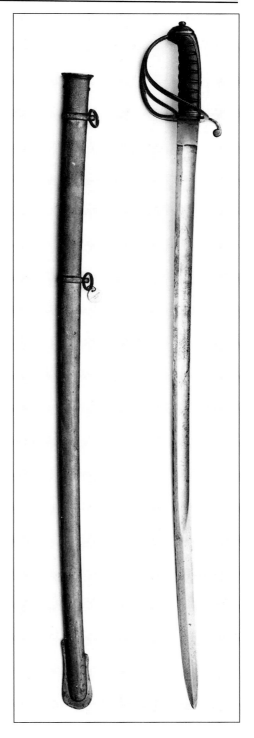

Light Cavalry officer's sword, pattern 1822; worn by Capt. Hutton, 4th Light Dragoons. (National Army Museum)

Heavy Cavalry officer's sword, pattern 1834; worn by Cornet Drury, 6th Inniskilling Dragoons. (National Army Museum)

lance was to be slung from the right arm, and when using the sword, from the left arm. In the attack both ranks were to carry their lances until the order to charge was given, when the front rank were to bring their lances down to the Front Guard; the rear rank were to continue at the carry but were to loosen their lances from the bucket. The lancer was advised to keep his enemy at a distance at all times, 'as the great advantage of the superior length of the weapon is lost as soon as the antagonist is able to close upon the lancer'. This point was highlighted by the ease with which the returning survivors of the Light Brigade managed to escape the intervention of the Russian lancers virtually unscathed. The lance was useless for picquet and outpost duties, and because of this the lancer still had to be provided with sword and pistol.

Light Cavalry trooper's sword, pattern 1829. (National Army Museum)

The Lance

This consisted of a nine foot long ash pole, impregnated with linseed oil and tar. The pointed steel head was attached to one end of the staff by rivets, and a steel shoe was fitted to the other end, which fitted into the leather bucket attached to each stirrup iron. A white buff leather arm strap was secured to the pole at the point of balance, by means of thonging. The lance was provided with a swallow-tailed pennon, 16 inches high by 27 inches wide, divided horizontally into equal parts, white over red.

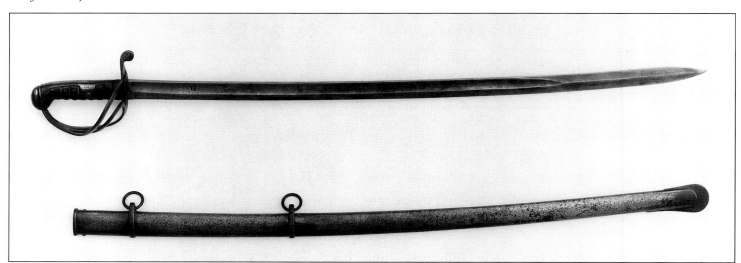

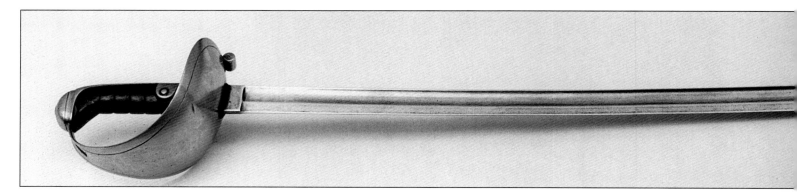

Heavy Cavalry trooper's sword, pattern 1822. (National Army Museum)

The Carbine Exercise

Carbine firing was carried out, at first, on foot, with blank cartridge, and then mounted, at the halt, and on the move.

The Cavalry Carbine

With the exception of Sergeant-Majors, Trumpeters, and all other ranks of the 17th Lancers, the cavalry was equipped with carbines which were carried on the off side, with the muzzle resting in the carbine bucket, the carbine strap round the small of the butt, and attached to the rider's pouch belt by means of the clip on the swivel.

The selection of a suitable percussion carbine for the cavalry had become a considerable problem in the years leading up to the Crimean War. During the general re-equipping of the army with percussion weapons in 1839-1849, George Lovell, Inspector of Small Arms, introduced the Victoria carbine, which was only issued to Heavy Cavalry. Somehow, and it is not clear why, its distinctive name was transferred to the cavalry carbines of the 1842 series, which came in two versions: a musket bore carbine with a 26-inch barrel for Heavy Cavalry, and a carbine bore model with a 21-inch barrel for Light Cavalry.

Cavalry trooper's sword, pattern 1853. (Mollo Collection)

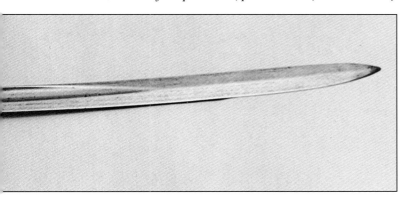

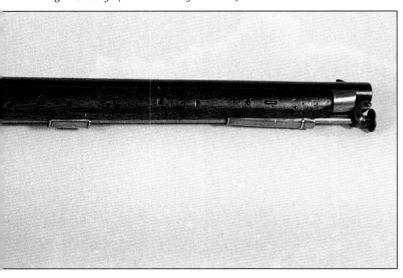

Victoria pattern carbine with swivel rammer for Heavy and Light Cavalry. (National Army Museum)

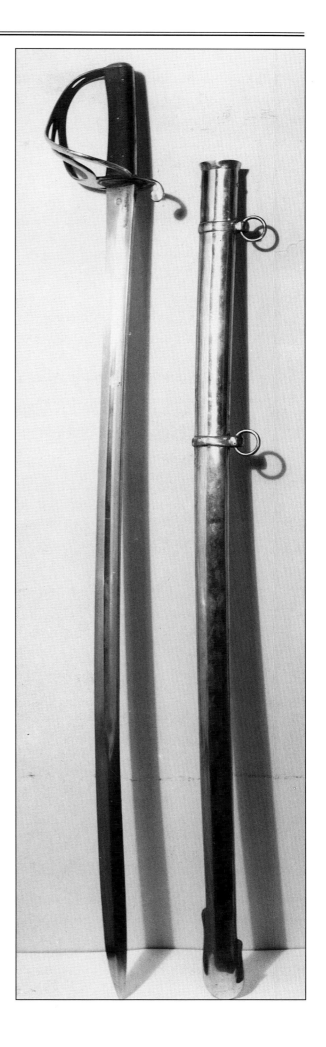

Officer's revolver, Deane Adams Model 1851, .50 calibre. (National Army Museum)

Cavalry trooper's pistol, pattern 1842, carried at Balaclava by Sgt. Wickstead, 5th Dragoon Guards. (National Army Museum)

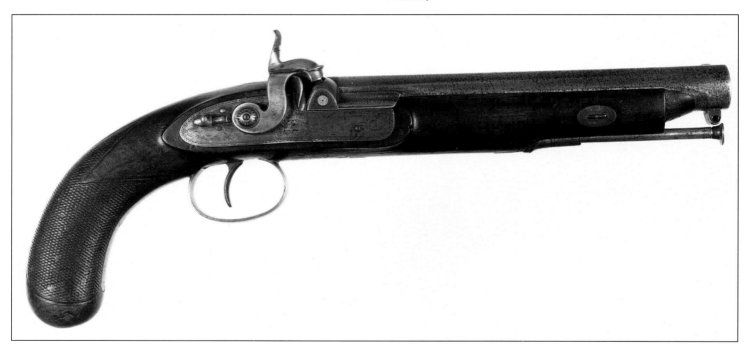

Pistols & Revolvers

Most officers purchased revolvers privately, the most popular being the Navy Colt and the Adams. The pistol for other ranks, which has been described as 'an extraordinary clumsy affair' had a nine inch long musket bore barrel, a musket lock, and a sharply cut down butt, ending in a flat brass plate. The pistol, held upright when drawn, in the same position as the sword at the 'carry', was an especially inaccessible weapon. In order to get at it the rider had to remove his right glove, push forward the cloak, or draw back the sheepskin and shabraque, and reach for the butt of the pistol, which was in the holster on the near side, hidden under his left hand.

Dress on Service

The cavalry regiments 'ordered to the East' left in a very slightly modified version of the full dress which had been essentially the same for the preceding quarter of a century. This full dress was described in the various regulations, amendments, and additions issued by Horse Guards; but for information as to how this peacetime dress was further modified, under the pressure of active service in a hot climate, there are only a few scattered references in diaries, letters, and memoirs, the Divisional Orders issued by Lord Lucan, and a small body of contemporary illustrations — notably those of Ebsworth, and the French General Vanson.

Leaving England

Before embarking their regiments, commanding officers made various attempts to prepare them for service. The shabraques of the officers of Heavy Cavalry, and all ranks of the Light Cavalry, were left behind. In their place the commanding officer of the 13th Light Dragoons provided all his men with sheets of black oil-cloth, which were to prove invaluable for a variety of purposes. The commanding officer of the Royals ordered his officers to leave behind their gold embroidered epaulettes, pouches, and belts, and his men their brass shoulder scales. The source of this information goes on to say that 'some other regiments' very sensibly replaced their shoulder scales with 'quadruple chains', as a protection against sword cuts. The swords themselves were, in the case of the 11th Hussars, sent to Dublin to be sharpened under the supervision of two officials from the Tower of London. White linen covers were provided for the various head-dresses, as a concession to the hot weather expected in Turkey.

In the Heavy Cavalry regiments, all ranks had their overalls 'strapped' with black leather, round the lower part of each leg and up the inside to the fork, to make them last longer; but there seems to be a question as to whether the Light Cavalry had these 'booted' overalls as well. Ebsworth shows the 13th Light Dragoons wearing them, in a sketch done as they were embarking; but Vanson shows all the regiments of the Light Brigade without them; and this is confirmed by the author of *Death or Glory Boys*, who states that the light grey trousers of the 17th Lancers were strapped with grey cloth, the booted overalls being adopted later in the campaign. Nevertheless some officers equipped themselves with reinforced overalls, notably Captain Hutton of the 4th Light Dragoons, and Cornet Wombwell of the 17th Lancers.

Trumpet-Major Harry Joy, of the 17th Lancers, recalled that, 'Just before sudden orders came for embarkation for the East some craze came over the authorities for alteration to cavalry equipment instanced by Captain Nolan's work on Cavalry dress proposed (grey overalls to wit), the shako or chapska was reduced in weight from 4 lbs which it weighed with cap cover . . . The extra men and broken up bands of the 4th Light Dragoons and 17th Lancers, were sent to Church St Barracks, Brighton, whence drafts (were) sent to (the) Crimea . . . '

Just prior to embarkation the men were issued with haversacks by the Ordnance Department; and once on board were issued with 'Sea Necessaries' consisting of the following items, which were specified for troops embarking for the Mediterranean, West Indies, and Cape of Good Hope:—

1 Canvas Frock.	1 Lb Soap.
1 Shirt.	1 Quart Tin-pot (with Hook).
Needles, Thread, Pipe-Clay.	1 Lb. Tobacco.

Sergeant Mitchell, however, describes a 'Sea Kit' of canvas slop and trousers, red worsted night cap, and two blue striped shirts.

The cost of these items was to be deducted from the advance of pay usually allowed to soldiers embarking for foreign service, but Private Thomas Davis, of the 17th Lancers, was not very happy about the arrangement. Writing from Malta on 6 May, he complained that 'they have given us out a slop suit that will be of no use to us when we go on shore and charges us 10/6 for them'. In fact the canvas frock was extremely practical and can be seen being worn at Scutari in some of the photographs taken by J. Robertson.

Turkey and Bulgaria

Once safely landed and settled into the barracks at Kulalie, Lord Lucan proceeded to issue a stream of orders to those regiments of his command that had so far arrived. His first order about dress, dated 29 May, complained about officers appearing in 'fantastical foolish dresses', the wearing of non-regulation sword knots, and the long hair and beards of both officers and men. In this last matter he was fighting a losing battle, for some eight weeks later all ranks of the Army of the East were permitted to grow beards and moustaches.

On 2 June detailed orders were issued about the packing of the Dragoon's baggage in marching order. In the near side of the valise were to be packed:

1 Pr Canvass Trousers.	1 Mug.
1 Shirt.	1 Knife.
1 Flannel Vest.	1 Fork.
1 Towel.	1 Spoon.
1 Pr of Socks.	1 Shoe Brush.
1 Holdall.	1 Clothes Brush.

And in the off side,

1 Pr Overalls.	1 Pr Drawers.

A packet of ammunition was to be placed at either end of the valise. For the rest, the forage cap was to be carried between the holsters; canvass frock, stabling jacket, and shoes 'under the pocket'; and the web surcingle and plume in the pocket of the valise. The camp blanket, issued on arrival in Turkey, was to be doubled, then folded in three, and laid evenly on top of the valise; the curry comb and brush were to be placed in the off side holster or wallet; and the corn-sack, with 24 lbs of barley evenly divided, was to be placed over and behind the cantle of the saddle. Two fore-shoes with nails were to be carried in the near shoe-case, and two hind-shoes with nails in the off shoe-case. The haversack, containing the mess tin, was to be worn over the right shoulder, falling to the near-side, and the water canteen, issued on arrival in Turkey, over the left shoulder, falling to the offside.

By now the white cap covers were in general use, General Vanson showing them being worn by the 11th Hussars and 17th Lancers, in particular: 'Nothing,' wrote Lord Cardigan, 'could render the entire Brigade more conspicuous than the white cap covers, with which all the regiments were equipped!' On 1 June a major concession was made when, in a General Memorandum, it was ordered that 'during the hot weather the soldiers will not wear stocks'. This must have resulted in a rash of fancy neck-wear, for four days later a further order pointed out that the abolition of stocks did not permit the soldiers to

'substitute Handkerchiefs for them'. They were to wear either their stocks or nothing, on parade, depending on the commanding officers. The custom, prevalent in the infantry, of turning down the high collar of the coatee, does not seem to have been permitted in the cavalry. Vanson shows them with their collars firmly hooked up, and stocks possibly being worn until after the date of the

battle. Assistant-Surgeon Cattell, of the 5th Dragoon Guards, recorded his regiment's arrival at Varna when they encamped on the beach and immediately put on their white helmet covers. He also states that the officers deposited their gold 'box epaulettes' at Hansen's Bank in Constantinople.

Officer and private, 17th Lancers, in review order; other ranks in marching order. Watercolour by R. Ebsworth from sketches made at Hounslow, 1854. (Bibliothéque Nationale, Paris)

(continued on page 116)

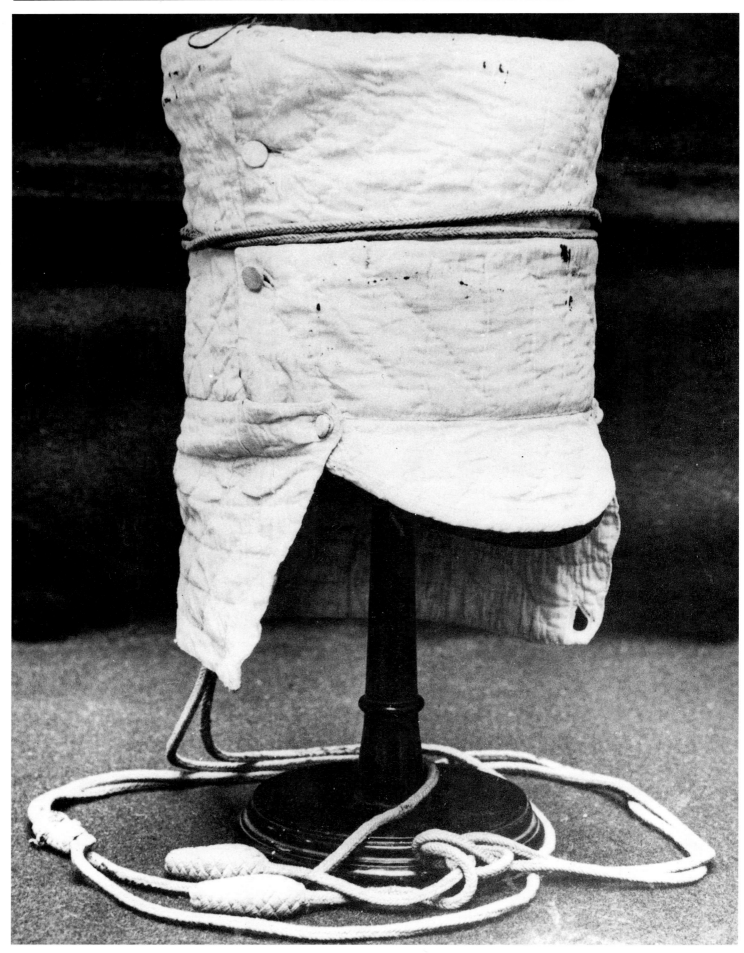

White calico cover for the Light Dragoon shako in hot climates, 1844-55. (Parker Gallery)

13th Light Dragoons, dismounted private in marching order, back view, 1854. Pencil drawing by General Vanson. (Musée de l'Armée)

8th Hussars private in stable dress, Varna, August 1854. Pencil drawing by General Vanson. (Musée de l'Armée)

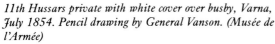

11th Hussars private with white cover over busby, Varna, July 1854. Pencil drawing by General Vanson. (Musée de l'Armée)

17th Lancers, service dress in camp; camp of the Light Brigade near Varna, August 1854. Pencil drawing by General Vanson. (Musée l'Armée)

On 27 June Lord Lucan, now in Varna, ordered that all officers, with the exception of the Regimental Staffs, were to provide themselves with spy-glasses, watches, and compasses, and were never to appear in marching order without them. On 8 August a further order listed the various orders of dress to be observed by the cavalry:—

1. Review Order.
2. Review Order with Baggage — As above but with valise.
3. Marching Order.
4. Field-Day Order — Stable-jackets, cloaks, arms, and belts, stripped saddles and gauntlets.
5. Drill order — Stable-jackets, stripped saddles, forage caps, arms and belts.
6. Riding School Order — Stable-jackets, forage caps, without carbines, pistols, or pouches.
7. Watering Order — Stable dress without arms or belts.

Except on Watering Parades, the collar chains were always to be worn.

On 10 August a further order of dress was introduced:—

8. Patrol Order — Field-Day Order, with the camp blanket rolled in three behind the saddle, and secured by the baggage-straps, and a shirt folded on the inside, the corn-sacks laid flat on the top of the blanket. One pair of shoes and two brushes in the wallets.

In the hope that the horses might be lightened by as much as two stone, this order of dress was to be preferred for all ordinary patrol duties, as the men could be sent so equipped on duties of even a week's duration. On 25 August the leather of the overalls was ordered to be kept oiled and blackened; and on the 27th all the regiments in the Division, 'with the exception of Lancers, who carry a pistol', were ordered to carry their shoes and brushes in their wallets.

On 30 August there was a long order in which Lord Lucan complained about the 'dirty appearance of the cavalry division', and ordered commanding officers to lay in a stock of 'yellow ochre and pipeclay, articles not

5th Dragoon Guards, escort of Lord Scarlet (sic), review of effectives, March 1855. Pencil drawing by General Vanson. (Musée de l'Armée)

4th Dragoon Guards, foraging order, camp before Balaclava, prior to 25 October 1854. Pencil drawing by General Vanson. (Musée de l'Armée)

5th Dragoon Guards, camp before Balaclava, prior to 25 October 1854; dismounted, in stable dress. Pencil drawing by General Vanson. (Musée de l'Armée)

5th Dragoon Guards, around 25 March (1855); dismounted, in marching order. Pencil drawing by General Vanson. (Musée de l'Armée)

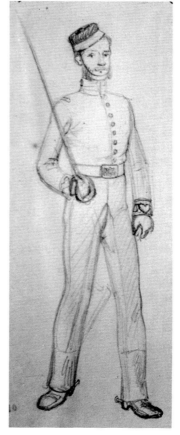

obtainable here'. The men were not cleanly in their appearance or in their persons; their clothes were dirty and stained; their arms dirty; and the belts, leathers, and appointments, both of man and horse, rusty and dirty. Commanding officers were dispensing with the use of 'oil, pipeclay, blacking, chrome, and everything else, without which it is unreasonable to expect a Dragoon to make a decent appearance'. A final order, issued from the steamship *Simla*, 'at sea', on 7 September laid down that all regiments, except Hussars, were to discontinue the use of sabretaches at once.

*2nd Dragoons (Royal Scots Greys), near Sevastopol, 19
October (1854); NCO mounted, in marching order. Pencil
drawing by General Vanson. (Musée de l'Armée)*

2nd Dragoons, officer in church parade order, March (1855). Pencil drawing by General Vanson. (Musée de l'Armée)

2nd Dragoons, trumpeter in church parade order, March (1855). Pencil drawing by General Vanson. (Musée de l'Armée)

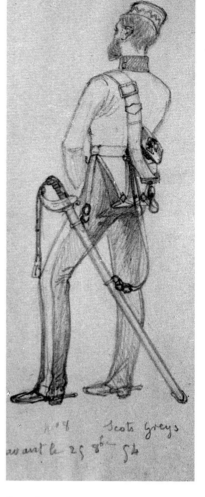

Scots Greys, prior to 25 October (1854); private dismounted, in stable dress, back view. Pencil drawing by General Vanson. (Musée de l'Armée)

2nd Dragoons (Royal Scots Greys), c1854; private dismounted, in stable dress, back view. Pencil drawing by General Vanson. (Musée de l'Armée)

The Landing in the Crimea

The Light Brigade was ordered to disembark in Patrol Order, but with dress jackets, without epaulettes and shoulder-scales, and with sheepskins. The stable-jacket was to be left behind. Twenty rounds of ammunition were to be carried in the pouches, and a further ten in the wallets. Sergeant-Major G.L. Smith, of the 11th Hussars, recalled that they were ordered to leave their pelisses and valises on board ship, and to take only one shirt, which was to be rolled in the blanket, and strapped on the saddle, in place of the valise. After the landing the haversack and canteen were both worn suspended from the right shoulder, resting on the left hip.

The Heavy Cavalry fared rather better, arriving later, and bringing their valises with them. Harry Powell, a Trumpeter of the 13th Light Dragoons, recalled the Scots Greys landing 'at a place one or two day's march from the Alma, horses and men looking as clean as if they were going to a review in Hyde Park; . . . we, poor dirty and ragged lot coming up, showed a marked contrast in our appearance'.

(continued on page 124)

13th Light Dragoons, camp near Balaclava, prior to 25 October 1854; dismounted sentry. Pencil drawing by General Vanson. (Musée de l'Armée)

6th Dragoons, near Balaclava, prior to 25 October (1854); private dismounted, in stable dress. Pencil drawing by General Vanson. (Musée de l'Armée)

4th Light Dragoons, Brigade Cardigan, the exact dress worn by the regiment at the battle of Balaclava, 25 October 1854. Pencil drawing by General Vanson. (Musée de l'Armée)

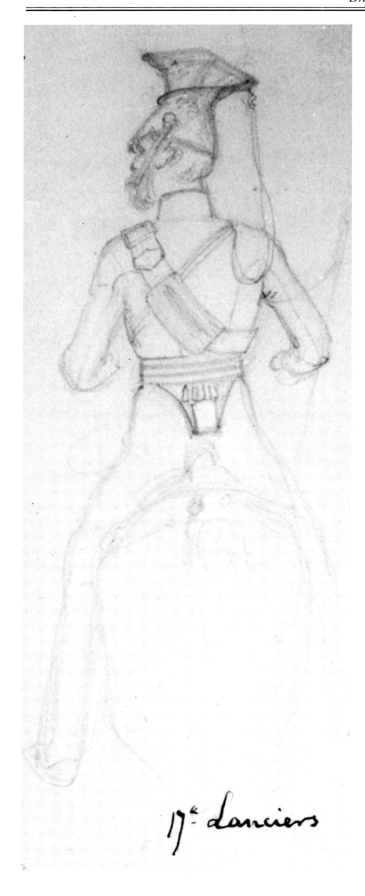

17th Lancers, mounted private in marching order; Balaclava, October 1854. Pencil drawing by General Vanson. (Musée l'Armée)

Unidentified officer, 4th Light Dragoons, spring 1855; mounted, in marching order. Photograph by Roger Fenton. (Parker Gallery)

17th Lancers, mounted private, back view; Balaclava, October 1854. Pencil drawing by General Vanson. (Musée l'Armée)

Balaclava

On 4 October it was ordered that no plumes were to be worn by the Heavy Cavalry on any occasion. On the 25th, the day of the battle, the cavalry turned out in Patrol Order, with haversacks and canteens, dress jackets, and the Heavies apparently without gauntlets. Assistant-Surgeon Cattell, who watched the charge of the Heavy Brigade from close by, and was on hand to help the wounded as they emerged from the mêlee, 'rushed forward, soon meeting some Inniskillings wounded in the sword arm, which the enemy (did they know we had discarded gauntlets?) had been taught to strike, with thumbs partially severed'.

The Light Brigade turned out in the same Order of Dress, with shakos and lance caps covered, but Hussar fur caps uncovered. In the Light Dragoons the officers had special foul-weather shakos, which looked like the full dress shako in a cover, but which were solid. The officers of the 17th Lancers had similar made-up foul-weather caps, but the surviving cap of Cornet Wombwell seems to have been a home-made affair consisting of an oilskin cover stretched over a light framework.

It was not until 12 November, when the winter had set in, that the regiments of the Light Brigade received their

Captain and Adjutant John Yates, 11th Hussars, in marching order. Photograph by Roger Fenton, spring 1855. (Parker Gallery)

valises, which they had left behind eight weeks earlier. During this period of time, Sergeant-Major Smith recalled, he had not had his overalls off once. The non-combatant author of *A Month in the Camp Before Sebastopol* summed up the state of the army in the following words: ' . . . it was the necessity, when they disembarked here, of bearing all their possessions on their backs, that reduced the Army to their worst trials. The suffering entailed by actual fighting, by night-work in the trenches, or by a bivouac such as the troops were only relieved from five or six days ago, are bad enough; . . . But the unmentionable horrors of a state of things where neither the clothing can be changed, nor the body cleansed, for weeks and weeks! — when men born and trained as our Officers are born and trained, are found undergoing these, without a complaint on their lips — England may well be proud of her "gentlemen".'

A sentiment which could equally well be applied to all ranks who served in the Crimea.

Cornet Henry Wilkin, 11th Hussars, in marching order.
Photograph by Roger Fenton, spring 1855. (Parker Gallery)

Bibliography

Adye, J.M.., *A Review of the Crimean War to the winter of 1854-5*, (London: 1860).

Almack, E., *The History of the 2nd Dragoons, Royal Scots Greys*, (London: 1908).

Anglesey, The Marquess of, FSA., *A History of the British Cavalry*, Vols 1 & 2, (London: 1973 & 1975).; (Ed.), *Little Hodge, being extracts from the diaries and letters of Colonel Edward Cooper Hodge written during the Crimean War, 1854-1856*, (London: 1971).

Atkinson, C.T., *History of the Royal Dragoons, 1661-1934*, (London: 1934).

Barthorp, M.J., *British Cavalry Uniforms since 1660*, (Poole: 1984); *The Charge of The Heavy Brigade*, Military Modelling, December 1985; *Crimean Uniforms: British Infantry*, (London: 1974).

Barret, C.R.B., *History of the XIIIth Hussars*, (London: 1911).

Blackmore, H.L., *British Military Firearms, 1650-1850*, (London: 1961).

Brereton, J.M., *A History of the 4th/7th Royal Dragoon Guards*, (Catterick: 1982).

Bushby, H.J., *A Month in the Camp before Sebastopol*, (London: 1855).

Cardigan, Earl of, *Eight Months on Active Service; Or a Diary of A General Officer of Cavalry*, (London: 1860).

Denison, Lt-Col. G.T., *A History of Cavalry from the Earliest Times*, (London: 1877).

Ffoulkes, C., and Hopkinson, E.C., *Sword, Lance and Bayonet*, (Cambridge: 1938).

Forbes, Major-General A., *A History of the Army Ordnance Services*, (London: 1929).

Fortescue, The Hon. J.W., *A History of the British Army*, Vol. XIII, (London: 1930); *A History of the 17th Lancers (Duke of Cambridge's Own)*, (London: 1895).

Gernsheim, H. and A., (Ed.), *Roger Fenton, Photographer of the Crimea*, (London: 1954).

Hibbert, C., *The Destruction of Lord Raglan*, (London: 1961).

Horton Major J., *The Evolution of the Cavalry Saddle*, The Cavalry Journal, 1909.

Jackson, Major E.S., *The Inniskilling Dragoons, The Records of an Old Heavy Cavalry Regiment*, (London: 1909).

Klembowsky, Col. W., *Vues Des Champs de Bataille de la Campagne de Crimée, 1854-1855*, (St. Petersburg: 1904).

Maude, Lt-Col. F.N., *Cavalry: Its Past and Future*, (London: 1903).

McClellan, Major-General G.B., *The Armies of Europe*, (Philadelphia: 1861).

Mitchell, Sergeant A., *Recollections of One of The Light Brigade*, (London: 1885).

Moyse-Bartlett, H., *Louis Edward Nolan and his influence on the British Cavalry*, (London: 1971).

Murray, The Rev. R.H., *The History of the VIIIth King's Royal Irish Hussars, 1693-1927*, (Cambridge: 1928).

Nolan, Capt. L.E., *The Training of Cavalry Remount Horses*, (London: 1852); *Cavalry: Its History and Tactics*, (London: 1853).

Paget, Lord George, *The Light Cavalry Brigade in the Crimea*, (London: 1881).

Parkyn, H.G., *Shoulder Belt Plates and Buttons*, (Aldershot: 1956).

Pomeroy, Major The Hon. R.L., *The Story of the 5th Princess Charlotte of Wales's Dragoon Guards*, (London: 1924).

Powell, H., *Recollections of a Young Soldier before and during The Crimean War*, (Oxford: n.d.).

Scott Daniell, D., *4th Hussars. The Story of the 4th Queen's Own Hussars, 1685-1958*, (Aldershot: 1959).

Scurfield, R., *British Military Smoothbore Firearms*, JSAHR, XXXIII, 159.

Smith, G.L., *A Victorian RSM, From India to the Crimea*, (The Memoirs of Sergeant-Major G.L. Smith, 11th Hussars), (Tunbridge Wells: 1987).

Strachan, H., *Wellington's Legacy, the Reform of the British Army, 1830-54*, (Manchester: 1984).

Tylden, Major G., *Horses and Saddlery*, (London: 1893).

Whinyates, Col. F.A., *From Coruna to Sevastopol*, (London: 1903).

Wilkinson-Latham, J., *British Military Swords from 1800 to the Present Day*, (London: 1966).

Williams, Capt. G.T., *Historical Records of the XIth Hussars, Prince Albert's Own*, (London: 1908).

Wood, General Sir E., VC, GCB, GCMG, *The Crimea in 1854 and 1894*, (London: 1895).